Chic & Slim
CONNOISSEUR

Chic & Slim Connoisseur: Using Quality To Be Chic Slim Safe & Rich
Anne Barone

Copyright © 2008 and 2013 Anne Barone

All Rights Reserved No part of this book may be reproduced in any form or by any mechanical or electronic means, including photocopying and recording, without written permission of the publisher, except in the case of brief quotations in articles or reviews and limited excerpts for personal use.

A Chic & Slim Book | Published by The Anne Barone Company

http://www.annebarone.com

Second Edition

Book Cover & Design: Anne Barone
Chic Woman Image: Copyright © iStockphoto/ karrapa
Book Cover Typography: Biographer Copyright © Sudtipos,
Rosedal © Del Alma, and Birch® Std Regular, a trademark of Adobe
Tower Design: Joyce Wells, GriggsArt

ISBN:Print: 978-1-937066-14-7
ISBN Kindle: 978-1-937066-13-0
ISBN ePub: 978-1-937066-15-4

Chic & Slim
CONNOISSEUR

Using
Quality
to be
Chic
Slim
Safe
& Rich

Anne Barone

Chic & Slim Readers Comment

Anne, I know you hear this constantly, but THANK YOU! You are a voice of sanity in a world of confusing dietary information. Ironically, I actually eat healthier following your advice than I do when I try to follow one of the latest nutritional diet gurus.

Thank you also for your information on living a simple, elegant life. In this country we seem to live with no concern for the rest of the world, and have excess and waste in every area from food to the homes we live in. Other books seem to stress either elegance OR simplicity, but you do a great job of combining the two. Anne, please continue to share your information. I'm not sure you realize how desperately it is needed today.

— **Cindy in South Carolina**

Thank you for writing this enchanting, exciting and totally delightful book. Bravo for all you have done. —**Jane in Vancouver**

Every summer I enjoy rereading the 3 books I have of yours—Chic&Slim, Encore & Techniques. Each time I read I'm in a different place in my own French Chic walk, and each year a different story or turn of phrase catches my attention. I read in my boudoir—a sitting area in my master bedroom, set apart by a Chinese screen—and these afternoon reads always leave my feeling happy and refreshed, because what you say is SO TRUE and what you recommend ALWAYS WORKS! *Merci encore, mon amie.*

—**Francesca, Moderator French Chic Board**

Ms. Barone: Your Chic & Slim philosophies are truly and authentically French.

—**Marilyn whose French mother is 84, still slim & beautiful**

Table of Contents

Author's Note

This *Chic & Slim* book had a previous incarnation when it was published five years ago as *The New Connoisseur*. In this new edition, the original text has been retained—but updated as necessary for better relevance to living well today. Additionally, new information has been added at the end of each of the four major sections. These additional 7700 words of new material are included to help you deal with recent challenges to using quality to be chic, slim, safe, and rich.

You, a Chic & Slim Connoisseur

Connoisseur:
one who possesses
knowledge and experience
to recognize true quality

Quality:
the excellence inherent
in an object or experience

QUALITY. What is the advantage of quality for you in these economically difficult times? In our perilous world, how can quality be your avenue to a chicer, slimmer, safer and richer life?

A decade and a half ago I published *Chic & Slim: How Those Chic French Women Eat All That Rich Food And Still Stay Slim.* More *Chic & Slim* books followed. Each book told women everywhere how they could be as chic and as slim as those much-envied French women. Those techniques are still useful. But today we have new challenges we must overcome to stay slim and maintain a chic personal style. Challenges to our personal safety and financial security are real and growing.

So how is a *Chic & Slim* Connoisseur different from the traditional connoisseur of vintage wines, Old Master paintings and haute cuisine?

First of all, wealth is not required. You can be a *Chic & Slim* Connoisseur no matter what your current income. *Chic & Slim* Connoisseurs use knowledge and experience to identify quality. They use quality to bring a level of richness, pleasure, happiness and success to their lives that no amount of money can buy.

Chic & Slim Connoisseurs use quality to make life the best possible—even in difficult and perilous times.

$\mathcal{S}tyle$ is the correct balance of knowing
who you are,
what works for you,
and how to develop your character.

Giorgio Armani
in *Self*

Audrey & Company

A Cinematic Connoisseur Perspective

ONE OF MY FAVORITE Audrey Hepburn films is *How To Steal A Million*. In this 1966 comedy caper Audrey Hepburn plays Nicole Bonnet, an elegant Parisienne who is certainly chic, slim and rich. And safe? Well, that is why Nicole needs the assistance of the charming investigator played by Peter O'Toole. The film provides a vivid cinematic portrait of a traditional connoisseur along with some hints about the *Chic & Slim* variety of connoisseurship I am advocating.

In the film's opening, we see Nicole's father, art connoisseur Charles Bonnet taking his bows at a Paris art auction. Up for sale is a painting from the renowned Bonnet Collection. Then we cut to Audrey Hepburn as the ultra-chic Parisienne in head-to-toe Givenchy zipping back to the Bonnet's art-filled Paris mansion in her snappy little red sports car. Charles Bonnet, played with arch comedy by Hugh Griffith, is a traditional connoisseur. But traditional with a twist. He is, as was his father, an art forger. The supposedly previously-unknown masterpieces that fill the Bonnet Collection were actually created in a secret studio in the Bonnet's Paris mansion.

Bonnet forgeries fool the experts. At least they have up until the point the story opens. Advances in technology and a scientifically trained investigator Simon Dermott played by Peter O'Toole may be about to expose the game.

Complicating the situation is an American millionaire art collector played by Eli Wallach. Davis Leland is obsessed with one of the fakes, a sculpture Charles Bonnet claims is the Cellini "Venus." The American has already bought a Lautrec from M. Bonnet.

When Nicole asks her father if he sold the American "your Lautrec, or Lautrec's Lautrec?" M. Bonnet answers, "Mine naturally. Are you saying mine is in any way inferior?" It isn't. As the detective Simon Dermott reports on his inspection of the van Gogh in the Bonnet salon: It is a great van Gogh. The viewer knows, however, it is not van Gogh's.

Nicole tries to convince her father that he cannot continue to create and sell fake masterpieces. He protests that he is not selling to poor people. He sells to American millionaires who, in any case, are more concerned about brands and labels than intrinsic quality. Quite insane, M. Bonnet thinks. Must be brain damage from some contaminant in the ink they use to print American money.

Connoisseurs. Counterfeits. Copies. Labels. Obsessed collectors. Possible brain damage from contamination. Investigations of forgeries, Need to leave one's native country to go elsewhere for a good life. Brand building. Intellectual property rights. Technology's challenge to the good life. Plot elements in this for-fun, mid-20th century film foreshadow our complicated consumerism 40 years later and the topics for discussion in this book.

How To Steal A Million makes statements on connoisseurship, inherent quality, respect for the classics, real vs. fake, Americans obsession with brands and labels, and natural human reaction. Did director William Wyler or his screenwriter Harry Kurnitz, or the writer George Bradshaw, on whose short story "Venus Rising" the film was based, foresee how consumers would have to confront the confusion of these issues in the early 21st century?

The Charles Bonnet the world sees is the traditional connoisseur in his palatial home overseen by his uniformed butler. The Bonnet Collection art hangs on the walls of the stately rooms and sits in alcoves on marble pedestals. But we, the film's viewers, can see another side to M. Bonnet's connoisseurship. A traditional connoisseur reveres and acquires objects created by others. But Charles Bonnet creates his own masterpieces. He has studied and gained the knowledge and experience and perfected his abilities until he can paint a van Gogh as well as Vincent van Gogh, a Lautrec as well as Toulouse-Lautrec.

For this personal effort to create the quality in his life, Charles Bonnet is equally a portrait of the *Chic & Slim* Connoisseur. The blurb on the back of the DVD edition of *How To Steal A Million* begins: The finer things in life are free (and sometimes fake)!

Free, yes, especially if you create them yourself.

The masterpieces in the Bonnet Collection have been created by the hands of Bonnet *Père et Fils*. There are no workshops where scores of underpaid workers labor in inhuman conditions to produce hundreds of fake masterpieces to be marketed by a greedy employer growing rich on the profits. In any case, most of the fakes the Bonnets have created are for their own pleasure.

For as long as I can remember and before, certain sidewalks in Paris have been lined with the work of artists selling copies (in varying degrees of exactitude) of paintings displayed in the Louvre and other Paris museums. No one had a problem with this. For as long as I can remember and before, a woman who could not afford couture design took a magazine photo of a Chanel or Dior or hot designer of the moment to her dressmaker to have a copy made. Or she might sew it herself. No one had a problem with this. Nor did anyone object when someone took a photo of a Tiffany or Cartier ring to their local goldsmith and asked him to reset some stones in the exclusive jeweler's design. Nor when someone told their local architect and interior designer that they wanted their new home to resemble one by a famous architect and decorated by a celebrity decorator featured in *Architectural Digest*. People wanted the pleasure and cachet of the good design. When someone in Peoria or Podunk copied a luxury design, no one screamed intellectual property theft.

Even a few years ago when sidewalk vendors began selling fake luxury brand handbags for $20 and $30 each, the most common reaction was an amused smile. The handbags were so obviously fake they were parodies of the luxury products they copied, having more in common with the James

Bond spoof *Austin Powers* than with the like-the-real counterfeit Guccis, Pradas, Vuittons flooding the market.

Today factories in China turn out copies of luxury brand handbags by the thousands that not even the experts at companies such as Gucci and Chanel can distinguish whether or not it is a counterfeit or one from their own production. These counterfeits are sold in Knock-off Centrals such as New York's Canal Street and Los Angeles' Santee Alley, as well as in immigrant markets around the world and by vendors on the Internet. They are showing up in upscale boutiques and in major retail outlets mixed with, sometimes replacing, the authentic brand products. International security experts assure us that profits from the illegal sale of these counterfeits go to organized crime and terrorists. Counterfeit sales that were previously amusing are now cause for real concern.

In *How To Steal A Million*, Nicole Bonnet struggles to convince her father that faking masterpieces is illegal. He dismisses the idea as a crazy notion his daughter has picked up in her job working with the Americans. The artists whose works he fakes are long dead. M. Bonnet points out that at the time of his death, van Gogh had sold only one of his paintings, whereas he, Charles Bonnet, has sold two van Goghs. As Charles Bonnet sees the matter, the famous Bonnet Collection serves as posthumous brand building on the deceased artist's behalf.

Nicole counters that selling fake masterpieces will eventually get them in trouble. She is right sooner than she imagined.

Counterfeits in the real world have caused problems for us sooner than we imagined. A savvy connoisseur must not only have the knowledge and experience to recognize and choose quality. They need the right information to make practical decisions in the pursuit of quality so as avoid eventual trouble.

Sometimes it is a choice between short term economy and long term security. The $100 counterfeit of the $800 handbag that is indistinguishable from the authentic may fit your budget. But it will prove a bad bargain if the profit from the sale of that counterfeit goes to train a bioterrorist who plants the contaminant in your city's water supply that makes you sick.

How do you know what is real and what is fake? How can you tell if the Prada bag in the upscale boutique is authentic? How do you tell if the DKNY dress you bought at mall department store is actually one made by DKNY? Or whether it is a knockoff slipped into the retail supply chain through an agent in Hong Kong? How do you know if that Retin-A you bought at the medispa where you have facials actually contains tretinoin, or if it is a counterfeit version made in an illegal factory in Mexico and smuggled into the USA in a shipment of bananas and distributed either knowingly or unknowingly by the pharmaceutical wholesaler? How can you tell if the music CD you ordered from a seller on Amazon Marketplace isn't a counterfeit whose royalties will never be paid to the musical group you want to support?

How do you know if those glucose test strips you picked up for your grandmother at the pharmacy are not a substandard counterfeit that will give an inaccurate reading and put her in the hospital? How can you make sure the toy you are buying for your toddler is not covered in lead paint? How can you know if those oranges labeled organic for sale in your supermarket were not grown in China where producers have been caught spraying their "organic" crops with prohibited pesticides? How can you make sure when you order fish in a restaurant that it was not raised in a polluted pond in Indonesia and contaminated with bacteria that will make you sick?

To find answers to these sorts of questions, a connoisseur must become a detective. In *How To Steal A Million* the investigator Simon Dermott who specializes in art forgeries holds degrees in both art and criminology.

You do not need degrees in fashion design and criminology to determine if the dress you are buying is a fake. Nor a degree in agriculture to determine if an orange has been grown with pesticides. What you do need is reliable information on which to make your judgment. You need techniques suggested in this book to find that information and learn how to distinguish between information that is essential and information that is unimportant or obfuscating.

Any connoisseur of chic would surely approve of the wardrobe Hubert de Givenchy designed for Audrey Hepburn to wear in *How To Steal A Million*. No detection needed here. These clothes are unquestionably authentic Givenchy. The ensembles the French designer created are my favorite film wardrobe for Audrey Hepburn.

The clothes she wore in *Charade* are also wonderfully chic. That evening dress she wore in *Sabrina* is unforgettable. But for sophisticated chic, no outfit Audrey Hepburn wore in *Charade* or *Sabrina* trumps that black cocktail dress with the veiled hat that she wears to meet Simon Dermott in the Ritz bar to plan stealing the Bonnet "Venus."

Perhaps the stunning dress keeps Simon from focusing clearly on the fact the elaborate theft for which Nicole wants his assistance (she has mistaken the investigator for a professional burglar) is to steal a statue that belongs to her family. He does finally question it. Nicole's indignant reply: "You don't think I would steal something that doesn't belong to me, do you?"

Nicole's integrity and ethics are as strong as her devotion to her father she is trying to save from exposure and certain imprisonment.

Integrity, ethics and efforts to keep oneself and one's family safe are also important traits for the *Chic & Slim* Connoisseur. The traditional connoisseur identifies high quality by the superiority of the materials, workmanship and design, and by the pleasure and good service it gives the user.

A *Chic & Slim* Connoisseur also judges quality by materials, workmanship and design, and by pleasure and service given. Yet for health, happiness as well as physical and financial security and quality of life, there must be additional standards by which she judges the quality of a product or experience.

In the following chapters we look at how a *Chic & Slim* Connoisseur identifies true quality and uses it to be chic, slim, safe and rich. Each goal is afforded its own chapter. In reality there are no definite demarcations between techniques for achieving those different ends. As I have been showing readers of the *Chic & Slim* books for years, an undeniable connection exists between your personal style and your ability to have a slim, healthy body. Techniques you use to choose quality for your personal style will also help you choose quality food that keeps you slim. They will also help you avoid possibly contaminated foods and consumer products that might injure you or make you ill. Those same techniques can save you time and money that will leave you a larger balance in your bank account. Chic. Slim. Safe. Rich. Like the links of the chain on a classic Chanel handbag, they are connected.

We begin with Chic.

Never use the word *cheap.*
Today everybody can look chic in inexpensive clothes
(the rich buy them too).

There is good clothing design on every level today.

You can be the chicest thing in the world
in a T-shirt and jeans—it's up to *you.*

Karl Lagerfeld
in *Harper's BAZAAR*

Connoisseur Chic

THE GIVENCHY DESIGNS that Audrey Hepburn wore in *How To Steal A Million* are incredibly and classically chic. They combine design, materials, and workmanship of highest quality. Quality has always been the foundation of chic. Buying quality for chic used to be simple. Now it is complicated.

It used to be simple to identify quality clothes and accessories and base our personal style wardrobe on them. But to be successfully and responsibly chic today, we must refine our definition of quality.

In today's global economy awash in counterfeits and substandard products, when multi-million dollar advertising sells aura of quality rather than true quality, it is often difficult to identify real quality. Even if you shop carefully, when you hand your credit card to the sales clerk, you have no guarantee that what you take home in the shopping bag will hold up through the season. A broken heel can have you hobbling for blocks. A seam that splits in public gives you a starring role in an unchic fashion disaster.

In the past, shopping for quality was simple because we knew the brands and could depend on them. We knew the stores, many still managed by the families that founded them. They did not disappoint. We knew the sales assistants who had worked in those stores forever. They knew us. They knew our personal style preferences. They knew our sizes, our budgets, and what our mothers or husbands would permit us to wear.

Now things are different.

The Handbag Question

While I was writing this book, I received an email from one of the *Chic & Slim* readers.

Anne, I received what I thought was a great handbag for Christmas, but it has not held up, and has proven not to be the best accessory choice for my small and carefully-crafted wardrobe.

I am getting paid on Friday, and don't have much extra cash, but I am absolutely willing to spend any (well, almost any) amount of money necessary to purchase a decent, chic, Parisian-style handbag—even if I have to order it over the internet and, alas, actually WAIT for it to get here!!

Could you please tell me, and your readers/followers, what a chic Parisian woman would do in this circumstance? I am not interested so much in a bag to take to market, but rather one that would serve me well in my profession as a legal analyst, in addition to looking chic enough for coffee or an art gallery during my time off with my boyfriend. Thank you! Darcy

While I do personally answer questions that arrive at *annebarone.com* via email, questions whose answers I believe will be useful to many readers, I usually answer in website postings or in the *Chic & Slim* books. In the following paragraphs I focus on handbags, but what I write about them applies to every category of item that we use to create our chic personal style: clothing, accessories, cosmetics, fragrance.

When I reflected on the problem handbag, to my mind, as likely to yours, came the possibility the handbag that had proved so unsatisfactory was a fake, a counterfeit purchased from a vendor selling counterfeits of luxury brands. No surprise if it fell apart. In that case, buying a quality handbag that would give long service would be a simple matter of not buying from an obvious vendor of counterfeits. Today, however, buying a quality handbag is more complicated.

Dana Thomas in her excellent *Deluxe: How Luxury Lost Its Luster* documents how today many luxury brand companies that once sold products created by careful craftsmanship and quality materials are now under the direction of businessmen whose only goal is profit. These well-known luxury brands use aggressive advertising to market the aura of quality. In fact, the products are now frequently made in China, or other countries with low wages, and are constructed of materials not to high quality standards that built those companies's reputations. Sadly, as we consumers have noticed, quality has deteriorated not just in many luxury items, but in every price range of apparel and accessories because of these same business tactics.

Other factors complicate the process of identifying and buying quality. Today buying from a major retailer or upscale boutique cannot guarantee that you might not buy a substandard fake. Counterfeit apparel and accessories are being marketed unknowingly by these retailers. The counterfeits are often found to have been slipped into the distribution system at transshipment points outside the USA.

Economist Pat Choate writing in *Hot Property: The Stealing of Ideas in the Age of Globalization* charges that some retailers knowingly mix counterfeit products with other merchandise. The huge quantity of counterfeits finding their way into stores is too great to be otherwise. "Many American retailers and importers make their stores available, blending legal and illegal goods on their shelves. Most of these retailers and importers are neither dupes nor victims. Inevitably, they know the source of their illicit goods."

For a better chance of avoiding disappointing purchases, a *Chic & Slim* Connoisseur must focus tightly on *real* quality. Quality for chic goes beyond design, craftsmanship and material. Also consider how well the item harmonizes with the wearer's personal style and body type. Women try on clothing and shoes, but often they forget to "try on" a handbag. They see a captivating full page ad for a handbag in a fashion magazine and forget that handbag is being shown on a model likely over six feet tall wearing five-inch heels. That same handbag carried by a five-foot, two-inch woman wearing her customary one-inch heels may not suit her so well. Other factors for quality consideration are whether the item gives service in balance with price, and whether is design provides both aesthetic satisfaction and pleasure of use. Handbag design is important for today's busy multi-tasked woman. We carry our lives in those bags. Well-designed compartments make the difference between organization and chaos.

If you are set on having a handbag bearing the logo of one the hot brands for which counterfeits exist, you can protect your investment buying it at a store with a good refund policy. An exchange is not acceptable if they just give you another counterfeit handbag that, like the first you bought, falls apart after a few months's use. You want your money back so you can buy a good bag elsewhere.

Not all counterfeits are shoddily made. But I hope that in your definition of quality you also take into consideration conditions under which many counterfeits are made. If their construction by children sold by their families to work under unhealthy and unsafe conditions does not offend your sense of common decency enough to keep you from purchasing counterfeits, I hope that at least you would have a strong enough sense of self-preservation that you would not buy a product whose profits may go to organized crime or terrorist groups, organizations aiming to do harm to you and your family. There is also the matter of counterfeits depriving the design's creator of income, a point more important perhaps to those of us who do creative work than to those who consume it.

Counterfeit Or Copy?

Of course you can always buy a good quality handbag made by a company not sufficiently "hot" that its designs and labels would be counterfeited. These handbags may be nearly identical to the design of those whose price and status make it profitable to counterfeit them. Keep in mind that just as a marked difference exists between a connoisseur and a mere collector, there is also a marked difference between a counterfeit and a copy.

Counterfeits mimic the design and carry the exact label of the original. Copies may mimic the design exactly, while materials and construction vary with price. Copies, however, carry the label of the company that actually produced and marketed the article.

A couple of decades ago, in a department store, I bought a handbag that copied exactly that classic bamboo-handled Gucci leather handbag. The moderately priced handbag made no claim of any association whatever with Gucci. It bore the label of whatever company made it. I have also owned a good copy of a "Chanel bag." Over the years, many of my handbags have mimicked the design of one luxury brand handbag or another. None were counterfeits.

In 21st century United States and Japan the handbag has claimed a position of unusual fashion prominence. These two countries account for about two-thirds of luxury handbag sales. If you have read *Deluxe: How Luxury Lot Its Luster,* you understand the corporate marketing strategies that created this buying obsession.

French Handbag Strategy

How important is your handbag to your chic appearance today? Since we often look to French women and their techniques for chic, I consulted that bible of French style *French Chic* by Susan Sommers. She wrote:

> Frenchwomen generally have one well-made handbag for winter, and another for summer, which take them through both day and evening. The quality is high, and so generally, is the price. But even when it is a bargain, it looks expensive. However this bag wears well for years and makes the owner look and feel wealthy.

Susan Sommers further tells us that the style and shade are neutral and size varies according to the wearer's needs.

Given that previous statistic on handbag sales in the USA and Japan, it seems safe to assume that chic French women have not become as obsessed as American women with the "It Bag" phenomena and are still following the system described in *French Chic.* That I have not observed the numerous pages of full page luxury handbag ads in French fashion magazines that I see in American fashion magazines seems to buttress my assumption.

Labels Aren't What They Used To Be

Fortunate are those who made their quality handbag acquisitions before outsourcing of production and designs reduced quality of materials and methods of construction. Those needing new handbags today can still purchase bags in good design and appearance and whose construction is in balance with price. Remember, however, in today's globalized world you can no longer depend on the label. (Take your lip liner pencil and write on your bathroom mirror: Today Labels Are Meaningless)

The Italians have the reputation for quality handbags that equals that of the French for perfume. Made in Italy on handbags (or shoes) long assured quality. Today, however, it is possible to manufacture a handbag (or any clothing item or accessory) in some low wage country, then ship it into Italy for some minor additional work, then label it Made in Italy and ship it into the USA. Some of the tricks manufacturers today perform in order to avoid telling you where a product was really made are truly amazing. Pat Choate's book *Hot Property* and Moisés Naím's book *Illicit* give details of these labeling subterfuges.

Perhaps even more than previously, it is a good idea to shop our own closets for quality items still serviceable. You might also check out closets of mothers, grandmothers and aunts. They might have stored a handbag that was "too good to give away," and would be delighted to pass on to you. Quality vintage is always in style. Having your own personal style based on quality rather than on the fashion *fad du jour* serves you well here.

In some parts of the USA, quality vintage clothing and accessories have so many pursuing them that they are difficult to find, and expensive when you do find them. In other parts of the USA where quality is unappreciated and only the trendy is valued, you can still make wonderful finds of quality vintage at yard sales and thrift shops.

Good News For Quality Chic

The factors that complicate buying a quality handbag today also complicate the purchase of quality in all the other elements of our chic. The good news is that there are still companies that make quality apparel and accessories. New companies are popping up. *The New York Times* reported on new designer jeans companies in the Los Angeles area. When major designer jeans companies moved their manufacturing operations outside the United

States, it left large numbers of skilled workers in this industry unemployed. One new company Bread Denim specializes in $200 vintage-washed, 100 percent organic cotton jeans giving employment to designer jeans skilled workers here in the USA.

Several months ago I received an email from one of the *Chic & Slim* Women who had been vacationing in Canada. She reported on Canadian clothing designers who were offering quality clothing designed and made in Canada. These designs were friendly to the bodies of "real women" that is, those of us who lack the height, emaciation and youth of today's fashion models. These Canadian designs were not cheap, she reported, but affordable and worth the quality of design, materials and construction.

Small fashion design companies, especially those dedicated to quality, usually lack advertising budgets to make the general population aware of their products. One blessing of the Internet is that we have more chance of learning about them than in a previous, more restricted media era. We can access the information through online discussion groups, blog postings and websites of design schools that feature career news about their alumni.

Affordable Quality Design

Chic depends as much on design as on materials and fit. For those of us whose budgets are limited, there is a recent helpful trend: "cheap chic collections." Created by name designers, these collections offer good design at prices far below those usually charged by the designer. The "cheap chic" line with which I am most familiar is the exclusive line for Target created by Isaac Mizrahi. I have been well pleased by the quality of design, construction and materials in all my purchases. I have been delighted by the low prices.

Karl Lagerfeld has designed a line for H&M. Other name designers have done budget lines: Vera Wang for Kohl's and Lela Rose for Payless

This democratization of fashion is good. Not only will it give many of us who could not afford a designer's more expensive clothes a chance to wear their designs, it can have other benefits. If more chic design is available at affordable prices, it may prompt women to update their personal style from those casual sweats so conducive to weight gain.

The traditional connoisseur buys expensive quality clothes in classic styles that last for decades. For the *Chic & Slim* Connoisseur, good design in less expensive quality may serve equally well. Perhaps better. Women today do not spend their lives in one lifestyle, nor one geographic region. Our moves take us from one climate to another. Chic in New York does not transplant well to Tucson. Certainly not to Miami or Stockholm. Women go from college student to gap year traveling the Amazon to corporate executive to stay-at-home mom doing part time consulting. What a woman wore in one role won't meet her chic needs in the next. The answer for many may be moderately priced good quality wardrobes that serve a lifestyle well a season or two and will not be a great financial loss when they are boxed up and sent to Goodwill the day before the moving van arrives.

When I lived in Corpus Christi on the Texas Gulf Coast, one day I walked into my favorite resale shop and the owner said, "Do you snow ski? If you do, I have bargains in your size." A woman who had recently moved to South Texas from Colorado had brought in several large boxes of very chic, obviously expensive ski wear. "She said they were taking up too much room in her closet and she wants to sell them." Clothes perfect for your lifestyle in one area may just hog closet space in another area. Also, many of us who have lived in humid, tropical climates and stored our "cold weather clothes" in a closet have learned, even with dehumidifiers and air-conditioning, we may still one day find that our black leather skirt and those boots that cost a fortune in that shop in London are victims of fuzzy green mold.

Chic Attitude Secrets

Chic today is as much defined by attitude as by clothes, accessories, and makeup. That confident chic attitude goes far toward convincing people we are attractive no matter what we wear. With a chic attitude, a woman wearing well-fitting budget jeans carrying a canvas shopping bag will turn heads when men won't notice another woman even though she is wearing jeans in the brand *du jour* and carrying this season's hottest luxury brand bag.

The tried and true confidence builders for a chic attitude have long been lingerie and fragrance.

Because lingerie is essential to that chic attitude, and because that chic attitude is so useful in our efforts to stay slim, I have been particularly annoyed to discover recently that the brand and style of lingerie I have been buying for years has undergone a dramatic decrease in quality. Annoyed, but not surprised. With more companies moving production to low wage countries and changing design and using cheaper materials in order to reap even higher profits, we see this decrease in quality in all types of consumer products.

In pursuit of quality, the *Chic & Slim Connoisseur* must accept that this trend of decreasing quality in many consumer products is only likely to continue. We have all read of an actress or society maven, learning that her favorite shade of lipstick or favorite cosmetic was being discontinued, bought up the company's remaining supply. If there are products which you could not live without if they no longer maintained their present quality, then, if you have the funds and the storage, you might want to buy a few extra to serve you until you could find a suitable replacement if necessary.

Sometimes, by the time you discover the product has changed, it is too late to buy extras. I used L'Oréal's Color Vive shampoo for so many years I cannot remember when I did not use it. No other shampoo made my hair look as healthy and pretty. Then, one day I went to the store to buy a new bottle. The familiar pearl white bottle was gone. Color Vive sat on the shelf packaged in a garish orange bottle. My heart sank when I saw the words "New Improved." They had changed more than the bottle. The first time I washed my hair, the after-shampoo results were very different from with the previous formula. The new formula also apparently contained an ingredient to which I am allergic.

Frantically I went from store to store looking for any Color Vive in the old formula not yet sold. No luck. But I did find a partially used bottle I had left in the guest bedroom bathroom at my mother's house. A quick Internet search lead me to a "natural" shampoo. Now my hair looks healthy and pretty again. I am actually happier using a product that contains (mostly) botanicals rather than chemicals. This replacement shampoo is more expensive than my former. Another fact connoisseurs must accept: we will likely have to pay more for products we find to replace those that change.

Fragrance: The Second Essential

The second essential for a chic attitude is fragrance. I queried the *Chic & Slim* website's fragrance authority asking if that important element in chic was also undergoing the same sort of downgrading of quality happening to clothing and accessories. Specifically I asked: How do the new fragrances created by companies such as Chanel, Dior, Givenchy, Nina Ricci compare in quality to the classic fragrances created by these companies? Dana Thomas describes in *Deluxe* how quality standards have been lowered for products such as handbags produced by luxury companies now under "business management." Does the price of these newly created fragrances reflect brand more than quality? The answer:

Dear Madam, There is no answer to this question. Many people have been educated or brain washed to like the new fragrances. When and if they get a chance to breathe in scents created by Serge Lutens or the Frédéric Malle line they usually say too strong not giving the fragrance a chance to weave its spell, which scent does over a period of time. Guerlain being sold to a conglomerate will eventually ruin the older fragrances because the company will try and find cheaper ingredients or tweak the perfume to be more modern. *Fleurs de Rocaille* by Caron & *L'Interdit* by Givenchy were ruined by modernizing their formulas.

Mitsouko is still a masterpiece along with these scents: *Après L'Ondée, Bellodgia, Bal à Versailles, Tabac Blonde, Chanel #5 eau de parfum*, Joy, *L'Origan* by Coty if you can find (Balanchine loved this scent). There are others but my memory has lost them.

The most beautiful and original fragrances can be found at Aedes de Venustas *aedes.com* Expensive one of a kind, mysterious, alluring perfumes will be here that are created & compounded like the great perfumes from long ago. At your service, Danny Morris

Aedes de Venustas (Temple of Beauty in Latin) is an elegant European style boutique in New York known for its niche fragrances and popularity with celebrities. Its website is an information-rich resource for someone looking for a special signature scent.

Choosing Your Signature Scent

I thought of those comments on the Serge Lutens and Frédéric Malle scents when I read Daphne Merkin's account in *The New York Times Style Magazine* about searching for her own signature scent and finding it in Carnal Flower.

Daphne Merkin wrote: "Six months ago I became enamored of one of Frédéric Malle's perfumes. I have never worn it and not been complimented on it or asked what I am wearing. I am convinced that I will go to my grave swathed in this fragrance."

Women email the *Chic & Slim* website and ask me how to choose a signature scent. If every time you wear it, you receive compliments on it, that is a strong sign you are on the right track. If you feel that you want to die wearing that scent, that is another sign. Fragrance, after all, is about how it makes us feel.

In pursuit of chic, women often give much attention to choice of clothing and accessories, but little to fragrance. Choose fragrance with much thought. As one French woman pointed out to me: No matter what you wear or what you take off, you are still wearing your fragrance.

Our *Chic & Slim* fragrance expert offered additional guidance to those choosing among fragrances for that special one:

So many of the fragrances now on the market, basically they are nearly the same with just a little bits & pieces of different ingredients added to veil their sameness.

A perfume has to have a linger quotient, that indefinable mystery that keeps you coming back to the fragrance. You may dislike the scent at first but the linger and dry down will seduce a person and cast its spell. That to me makes a great perfume.

A woman of great elegance always chose her personal perfume and this was her signature. All this advertising and advice that you should have a wardrobe of scents defeats the purpose of having your own fragrance. When you fall in love with your choice which has woven a soul quickening in your response to the fragrance, then reach out with an inner guidance of your soul and guard it with your heart. — D.M.

Today many fragrance companies try to convince us that we need a wardrobe of scents. This is marketing, not good advice for chic. Your fragrance is as distinctive to you as your face or personality. Frequent switching is counterproductive to chic. Quoting again from that bible of French style *French Chic*:

> Frenchwomen are faithful to their fragrance and use their personal scent as a signature, one with which they are associated and by which they are remembered. They do, however, experiment, and sometimes become so carried away by a new perfume that they fall captive to it and make a change. But they often stay with the same one . . . or two . . . for life.

Traditional connoisseurs define quality by design, materials and craftsmanship. *Chic & Slim* Connoisseurs perfecting their chic personal style in today's globalized world have additional considerations for the definition of quality: conditions of manufacture, possible effect on national and personal safety and how well an item serves their lifestyle needs.

Wholesale takeover of the purveyors of chic by those more interested in profit than quality, and who use aggressive marketing to give an aura of quality is troubling. As a *Chic & Slim* Connoisseur, keep in mind:

If we accept the reduction in the quality of apparel and accessories as placidly as Americans in recent decades have accepted the reduction in the quality of food items, it will become as difficult and expensive in the USA to buy quality to make us chic as it is difficult and expensive today to buy quality food products to keep us slim.

Connoisseur Chic Today

YOU WOULD HAVE THOUGHT they had gotten the message. Despite all the books, media articles, and television exposes, women are still buying counterfeit designer handbags and other fashion apparel thinking they are purchasing the real thing at bargain prices. In June 2011, *New York Magazine* published an article "Highly Convincing Counterfeit Handbags Are Severely Embarrassing Innocent, Bargain-Hungry New York Women" writing: Women all over the city are increasingly duped by what they think are real bags being sold second-hand for an astounding bargain.

And there are a LOT of counterfeit handbags out there. As recently as this past September, one St. Louis woman was sentenced to almost five years in prison for selling counterfeit Hermés handbags she purchased from a manufacturer in China and sold on her three websites. The FBI reported that it was a profitable business for her, netting over a half million dollars in sales in 13 months.

The bottom line seems to be that if you find a supposedly used designer handbag at a bargain price on the Internet or at a resale shop, likely it is counterfeit. If you want an authentic designer handbag, you will have to purchase it from the designer's own store, or from a store authorized by the designer. If your budget is limited, like chic French women of modest means, you may have to save for years in order to buy the designer handbag of the quality you desire.

Not Just Luxury Handbags And Apparel
But the deluge of counterfeits flooding the markets these days are not just

designer apparel and accessories. Counterfeits of all sorts are easily found at flea markets, small shops, and swap meets. Christmas lights, batteries, and toys cause particular concern. These poorly made fakes are dangerous. Improperly made Christmas lights can start fires, batteries can explode, toys have lead paint or parts that can injure.

As with evaluating designer items, to spot a counterfeit, examine the quality of materials used in the product and keep an eye out for misspellings on packaging or weird grammar in the instructions. The good news is that since 2009, US Customs is doing an increasingly better job intercepting counterfeit merchandise before it reaches retail.

Good News For Quality Chic

That "Good News For Quality Chic" that I reported in the first edition of this book, is even better news for quality chic today. First Lady Michelle Obama has been indefatigable in introducing little-known emerging designers by wearing their designs for important events. This effort began in Chicago even before her husband Barack Obama became a presidential candidate. She wore dresses by designers such as Isabel Toledo, a designer who received even better exposure when Michelle Obama wore her yellow ensemble at the 2009 Inauguration.

When Michelle Obama wore Jason Wu's inaugural ball gown in 2009, he was little known. By the time she wore another of his ball gowns for the Commander's ball in the 2013 Inauguration, Jason Wu was a well-known designer who has a secondary fashion line as well as shoe and handbag designs. He has also created an affordable collection for Target. His is just another in the expanding number of "budget chic" lines by talented designers that are making it possible for women to dress stylishly even in these more difficult economic times.

Like chic French women, Michelle Obama often mixes high and low fashion as when she puts a J. Crew belt with a Thom Brown tailored coat or wears an economical cardigan to top a designer dress.

Many fashion experts comment on the fact that because of Michelle Obama's size (she is fashion model tall, she is *not* fashion model thin) and the fact that she chooses many outfits that are within middle class budgets, many women can relate to her choice of fashions. While many of her fashion choices are modestly priced, she always chooses good quality. Michelle Obama provokes criticism, however, from those whose believe a US president's wife's fashion should run more toward classic design and neutral shades instead of the bright-colored patterns and prints in which she is often seen. In any case, many who think those styles and colors look fine on Michelle Obama simply do not have her height, her well-toned arm muscles, nor skin tone to wear those same styles and colors she favors.

Whether or not we would make the same fashion choices as Michelle Obama, we must give her credit for being a role model for how one develops a personal style uniquely suited to showcasing one's own personality. A personal style that also accents the body's best features and hides less flattering ones. Viewers focus on the toned arms and don't notice so much the broad hips under the full skirt.

Quality Fragrance Perils

True, the possibilities for quality chic clothing and accessories are better than when I wrote the first edition of this book. Unfortunately challenges face those who seek a quality fragrance. And not just the challenges that were outlined in the first edition of this connoisseur book.

Today counterfeits of popular fragrances are available almost everywhere—certainly online. But it is absolutely necessary that you learn to identify and avoid buying and using a counterfeit fragrance. *Harper's Bazaar* took the lead in the campaign against counterfeit fragrance. What they discovered was disturbing. In the magazine's 2010 article "The Fight Against Faux Fragrances," Maria Ricapito wrote:

> Wasting your money on a street Goyard tote may hurt your wallet when the flimsy strap snaps, but it's unlikely to physically harm you. Counterfeit perfumes, however, suddenly seem to be everywhere — at flea markets, on street-side tables — and they can actually make you sick.

> These counterfeits of expensive fragrances have been found to contain

urine, bacteria and antifreeze. Little surprise that when many women open the package of a counterfeit fragrance, they comment that it doesn't smell like the fragrance its package proclaims it to be.

As Valerie Salembier, senior vice president and publisher of *Harper's Bazaar*, told ABC News: "You're putting something on your face, on your neck, on your wrists. Those are sensitive parts of the body, so, to have active ingredients that could endanger your life is a very serious health risk."

In fact, reactions to counterfeit fragrances with dangerous ingredients have been found to cause redness, itching, runny nose and eczema. And, frankly, I don't want to know what long-term problems some of those dangerous ingredients in counterfeit fragrances might be causing women who absorb those ingredients into their blood stream on a daily basis.

In any case, for counterfeit fragrances as for other counterfeit items, if you buy them, because counterfeits are generally linked to organized crime and illegal activity, you are supporting gangs, drug and arms dealing—and perhaps, worst of all—terrorism. So if, as French women have long believed, that the value in fragrance is how it makes you feel, how do you feel about yourself if you are perfuming with a contaminated faux concoction whose profits go to support crime and terrorism?

If counterfeit fragrances are so widely available, how do you spot the fakes? The *Harper's Bazaar* article on faux fragrances gave tips. First, check the color. Too pale likely means lots of alcohol. Too dark color suggests impure or substituted ingredients not in the real version. Check labels. Poor printing or misspellings are always signs of counterfeit. The barcode should be on the bottom of the package, not the side of the package. Furthermore, if you find the luxury fragrance for sale in a flea market, from a street vendor or online vendor—except for Sephora or the websites of major department stores—it is likely counterfeit. Bargain price is always a tip off. No one is going to sell authentic luxury fragrances for a fraction of retail price. They can't pay the wholesale price of a legitimate fragrance and still make a profit.

On the other hand, I suspect that, other than the legitimate sales points such as Sephora or major department websites, today full retail price or authentic-appearing packaging is no guarantee of authenticity. Counterfeiters are not dumb. When the media began reporting on how to spot counterfeit fragrances, I suspect many counterfeiters decided to upgrade the packaging and raise the price to make their counterfeits appear more authentic. Testing my theory, I did online searches for several luxury fragrances and found numerous bottles listed for sale for full retail price from iffy sources.

An additional challenge to fragrance has grown more serious in the past five years. For those of us now 50s and older, those fragrances that we defined as our signature fragrance in our 20s or 30s, many are today difficult to find even at full retail price from the makers themselves. Some of the most-loved fragrances have been discontinued. For example, the original Rochas *Femme* created in 1944 is only a memory to those of us who loved wearing it—and those who loved that we wore it. Sadly, the Rochas *Femme* of 1989 had little similarity to the original.

Today new fragrances are created in such quantity and appear and vanish with such rapidity that for many of us it hardly seems worth the effort to identify the perfect new signature fragrance. If you do decide for one reason or another that you want to choose a new fragrance, an excellent resource is the United Kingdom-based *www.basenotes.net*. (Note this is .net, not .com). Here is everything you could possibly want to know about fragrances current or past. All fragrances cataloged in Basenotes' extensive database feature an ingredient list, a big help in finding a new fragrance when you know what ingredients created your previous favorite fragrances.

Quality: The Necessary Foundation For Chic

As always, today quality is the foundation for chic. Because quality lasts, and because a savvy connoisseur knows quality is not always directly tied to price, in the long run quality chic is never as expensive as one might imagine.

Food is Destiny

It turns out that Jean Anthèlme Brillat-Savarin was right in 1825 when he wrote in his magnum opus, *The Physiology of Taste*, that "the destiny of nations depends on the manner in which they are fed."

.... Food is destiny, all right.

Every decision we make about food has personal and global repercussions. By now it is generally conceded that the food we eat could actually be making us sick.

But we still haven't acknowledged the full consequences — environmental, political, cultural, social and ethical — of our national diet.

Alice Waters

Slow Food Nation *The Nation*

Connoisseur Slim

AT ALMOST THE SAME time that icon of chic slimness Audrey Hepburn, along with Peter O'Toole and the cast and crew, were in Paris filming *How To Steal A Million*, a young woman from California arrived in Paris to study at the Sorbonne. This Food-Connoisseur-To-Be never made it to her first day of classes at the historic university. She and her two roommates first ventured out to a Paris *pâtisserie* for hot croissants and *pain au chocolat* and brought them back to their apartment. Happy in breakfast nirvana of French pastries and *cafe au lait*, the young American women skipped class.

The story of Alice Waters' discovery of French food and lifestyle, and the American food revolution she has championed these past several decades is told in Thomas McNamee's *Alice Waters and Chez Panisse: The Romantic, Impractical, Often Eccentric, Ultimately Brilliant Making of A Food Revolution*. For those of us who, like Alice Waters, discovered French food and French *savoir vivre* in the mid-1960s, the book makes delicious and nostalgic reading. How well I understand when Alice Waters said:

> When I got back from France, I wanted hot baguettes in the morning, and apricot jam, and café au lait in bowls, and I wanted a café to hang out in, in the afternoon, and I wanted civilized meals, and I wanted to wear French clothes. The cultural experience, that aesthetic, that paying attention to every little detail—I wanted to live my life like that.

Many of us who grew up in 1950s America and who, like Alice Waters, experienced France in mid-1960s wanted to continue to live our lives *à la française*. We wanted to enjoy wonderful food and a pleasurable lifestyle even after we left France. We especially wanted to enjoy that rich French food that would keep us French slim to wear those chic French clothes. It was easier then than it is today.

The Secret: Quality

Quality was the French secret. Our experience taught us that important lesson. Not surprising that the word connoisseur that we English speakers use to denote a person who recognizes and uses quality is a French word.

In everything from the bread sold in the *boulangeries* to the kitchen gadgets in Monoprix, the French seemed to have only one quality: good quality. Their insistence on quality and attention to detail to achieve quality made everything from their personal style to their social interactions to their meals successful. The side benefit was delicious pleasure. The French took time and care with whatever they did in order to achieve the highest possible quality. They didn't do anything in a rushed, haphazard way. Well, except drive. Fortunately, in those days many French did not own cars.

From personal experience with food growing up in the USA, I knew that what had made the difference was not the absence of quality food products here. Instead, it was the manner in which food was prepared, the attitude toward food and eating, the manner in which food was eaten and the attitudes toward work and pleasure and life in general that made the difference in whether or not the end product was high quality.

When I was growing up in the USA in the 1950s and early 1960s, there was still much high quality locally produced food available. Certainly there was in that small town in Oklahoma in which I grew up. Despite the low annual rainfall, despite the hard red clay soil, gardens and orchards flourished. While neither my mother nor grandmother were gardeners, fortunately we had many friends and family members who were, and who shared generously.

The trend in the USA at that time might have been toward more convenience foods. But homemakers had not forgotten the more labor intensive techniques for creating from-scratch dishes, especially desserts.

My mother would use her electric mixer for whipping egg whites for an angel food cake. But she would tell you about how as a teenager she did the job with two forks. I believed her. But as long as the Sunbeam worked, I wasn't about to try it.

Comparing Food Habits

One difference apparent in the comparison of American and French food habits was that the French ate in courses, at least three, sometimes five per meal. Except breakfasts which were those lovely bowls of coffee laced with steaming milk eaten with bread warm from the bakery spread with fruit jam and butter. By the 1950s Americans, however, had demonstrated a decided preference for one-dish meals. Misnamed with the French word casserole (in French a saucepan) these were often concocted of instant rice, canned vegetables, canned chicken or tuna and canned soup. Campbell's Cream of Mushroom was a favorite choice. These meals in one dish were usually baked in a rectangular Pyrex, or later, CorningWare baking dish. Often the meat/veg/starch/soup was topped with shredded faux cheese.

But not everyone depended on canned products to produce those one-dish meals. The one my mother always prepared when she needed to serve a hearty meal that could be prepared ahead of time was Baked Chicken Spaghetti. The chicken that served as the basis of this dish was never from cans. Often it was a plump old hen raised and dressed by my stepfather's mother on the family farm. That farm, by the way, was also our source of pastured beef, fresh milk, eggs and hand-churned butter, as well as vegetables, and fruits. My lifelong passion for melon began the summer they planted cantaloupe in the wheat field nearest Red River. More than a half century later, I remember the extraordinary sweet taste of those cantaloupe. When the French would sing praises to their beloved Cavaillon melon, I would just smile. I knew Cotton County could do well in the melon department too.

Tomato juice used in my mother's Baked Chicken Spaghetti might come from a store can, but I remember times when the juice was poured from a quart glass jar of home-canned juice "put up" as the parlance went, by a generous friend or family member from ripe garden tomatoes. Celery, onions, and green pepper were always fresh, bought at a grocery store. Of course the olives and mushroom soup were from a can, and the spaghetti from a box.

Change & Natural Reaction

Yet in those days products found on the food store shelves were different from those we find there today. In the 1950s and for a time afterward, even those items in cans and boxes on the store shelves were plant and animal products people had been eating for centuries, if not millennia. The food industry meanwhile was beginning to change that. With no thought to quality and all thought to profit, food companies began to process food with chemical additives (and even some natural substances), that no people on earth had ever included in their diet. Naturally, some people were unhappy about that.

Some of the negative reaction was lead by people like Alice Waters and her cohorts as well as others of us, veterans of happy experiences with real food in Europe and elsewhere. All that food processing and additives were unacceptable to us because they degraded taste and nutrition. Natural food was needed for healthy bodies.

Groundwork that laid the foundation for the natural foods movement had been done in the 1960s by a colorful outdoorsman Euell Gibbons. His book *Stalking the Wild Asparagus* on how to recognize, gather and prepare natural foods was an instant bestseller. I recall that his recipe for pork and day lily buds was one of my more adventurous early natural food experiments.

For the less adventurous who did not want to stalk their food, even friendly wild plants, a host of natural foods cookbooks based on purchased ingredients began to appear. Banished from the recipes were the can of this and package of something else that were standard in popular cookbooks of the 1950s and 1960s.

For instance, my 1968 *Better Homes & Gardens* cookbook recipe for Rum Muffins calls for canned mincemeat and apple juice added to an orange muffin mix. And rum? Only 1/4 teaspoon rum *extract*. This is a family cookbook.

The new natural foods cookbooks one-dish meals replaced meat with nuts and whole grains, and processed ingredients with fresh. A natural casserole might contain celery, onions, carrots, cashews, brown rice, wheat germ, cottage cheese, fresh chives, sesame seeds, seasoned with sea salt, fresh parsley and thyme. No canned soup.

Natural foods stores opened to sell natural products not found in supermarkets. Homemakers tossed their boxes of instant rice and instant mashed potatoes and dipped into bins of soy grits, hulled millet and buckwheat groats. They loaded shopping baskets with produce grown without chemical fertilizers and pesticides. They switched to more natural sweeteners such as raw honey and blackstrap molasses. People who had never seen a tomato on a vine planted backyard gardens. Bread baking classes enrolled the willing. Some even bought home mills to grind their own bread flours. Fruits and vegetable juicers hogged space on kitchen counters. Mung beans and alfalfa seeds spouted in special dishes in dark kitchen cupboards to be discovered by startled, unsuspecting husbands looking for a beer mug.

The Food Industry Fights Back

This natural foods trend to take Americans back to the pleasure and healthier nutrition on which the human body had depended for millennium was a positive one. Ultimately, however, this natural foods trend was pushed out of the mainstream by stronger forces.

Among these forces was legislation that favored agribusiness, the persuasion of high-dollar advertising, Americans' own willingness to believe nutritional hype and a cultural tendency to want everything quick and easy. Another force was a new home appliance.

In the 1980s everybody bought a microwave and started zapping frozen commercial dinners and reheating carry-out. For many there was no going back to cooking real food in a kitchen and consuming it around a family table. By the end of the 1990s, many Americans had deserted the home dining table and were eating most meals in front of TVs, standing at the kitchen counter, in restaurants or in fast food outlets. An alarming number were eating while driving their vehicles.

Lessons Learned, Future Battles

Why have I taken you on this mini-tour of those thrilling days of gastronomic yesteryear in this chapter dedicated to staying slim?

For a good reason. I wanted to provide the culinary landscape as backdrop for another evolution taking place. During this time in which Americans increasingly gave up real food for food products largely based on some manipulated form of corn, wheat, or soy, with some unpronounceable chemicals thrown in, when they began eating in increasingly stressful environments, when the producers of food were less and less the small farmer and more and more huge agribusiness operations, Americans grew fatter and Fatter and FATTER!

If *Chic & Slim* Connoisseurs want to stay slim in the current food environment, we must become savvy. We must be alert to forces working to make us fat. In the USA today, putting quality food on our tables that will keep us chic and slim will take effort. For some, much effort.

Depending on where you live and how much time and money you have available for food shopping and preparation, the experience can vary from a pleasant promenade through a garden of delicious choices to a quixotic quest in a wasteland of tasteless, nutrition-robbed, "edible food-like substances" to use author Michael Pollan's phrase.

Food shopping for me today in North Texas is depressing. The often quoted line in "The Rime of the Ancient Mariner" comes to mind "Water, water, every where, Nor any drop to drink." Walking the aisles of my supermarket, I am inclined to paraphrase: "Food, food everywhere, but not a bite to eat." An exaggeration? *Bien sûr!* Yet most food products sold by my supermarket for one reason or another I do not eat. Some are purchased only because I have to eat and lack the time and money to purchase food of a more desirable quality.

For me, finding healthy, good tasting food for three meals a day, seven days a week takes far more time and money than I have ever before had to devote to the effort. The irony is that I live in a small North Texas city surrounded by agricultural production. A major wheat farming area lies to the north, an area of dairy farms can be found a few miles to the south, and fruit and vegetable production 20 miles to the east. Perhaps I would not mind so much, but for most of my life I have enjoyed reasonably easy access to quality food. When you know good food, and have become accustomed to eating good food, its absence becomes a particular reason for unhappiness. Especially when you know how poor quality food can make you fat.

The Real Danger

These past few years we have been so focused on the threat from foreign terrorists, that we have neglected to recognize that dangers lurking on supermarket shelves and fast food trays likely pose a greater threat to our health and safety.

In the current food era in which we find ourselves, for most people in the USA, agribusiness and the food industry provide most of their food. At the same time, we have entered an era of globalization. Increasingly what we find on supermarket shelves and in freezer cases are foods that have been grown and processed outside the USA. Or at least contain an ingredient that has been grown or processed outside the USA where sanitary and safety procedures may or may not be followed and enforced. These are also countries where foods tainted with carcinogens, bacteria, and poisons are common. Food processing today is not so much about processing as about assembling ingredients from whatever source in the world provides the cheapest.

The Tainted Food Problem

The chief source, but not the only source, of our concerns about contaminated food imports is China. Recent media reports have been frightening. Dried apples preserved with a cancer-causing chemical, frozen catfish laden with banned antibiotics, scallops and sardines coated with putrefying bacteria and mushrooms laced with illegal pesticides. Despite these widely reported problems and evidence of our government's inability to intercept contaminated food products coming into the USA, food imports from China are increasing. *The New York Times* reported in October 2007 that China's food and agriculture exports to the USA were up 27 percent over the preceding year, up to $2.5 billion. "Even in categories hit by high-profile recalls this year, like food and toys, exports rose sharply, according to data compiled by Global Trade Information Services, based in Columbia, S.C."

This means that more food in your supermarket will have been grown or processed in China. And yes, the Chinese government is taking steps to make the food they export safer. But given the level of environmental pollution in that country and the distance food must be transported from there for our consumption, it is hard to see how any food grown in China could meet a *Chic & Slim* Connoisseur's definition of quality. I certainly do not want to put into my body any food grown or processed in China, or in a number of other countries from which large amounts of food imports have been found to be tainted.

To make informed decisions about food of sufficient quality to keep us healthy and slim, one important piece of information we need is the country of origin. That information is surprisingly difficult to get.

We need implementation of COOL, the Country-of-Origin Label law passed as part of the 2002 Farm Bill. Various opponents, chiefly Congressional, have managed to delay implementation of this law requiring that beef, pork, lamb, fresh fruits and vegetables, seafood and peanuts be labeled to tell consumers the country in which they were produced. Only COOL labeling on seafood is now enforced. My own personal experience with the seafood counter in my supermarket is that the labeling provided is often unreliable. The portable labels are not always with the correct fish. Employees cannot answer questions about the source of the fish they are selling, even the simple question of whether the fish was shipped fresh or frozen.

European Solution

Europeans generally are better able to identify the source of foods for sale in their markets. As I told you several years ago in *Chic & Slim Encore*, the French and other Europeans are demanding to know where their food products are produced, not just what region, but on what specific piece of land the wheat for the flour or the vegetables and fruits were produced. In addition to EU regulations, businesses are responding to this demand. *Business Week* reported in a July 2007 article "Not Made In China:"

> After outbreaks of Listeria bacteria and other tainted food in Europe, French hypermarket chain Carrefour created Quality Line products, which come from local farmers who have agreed to tough quality standards. The products are now offered in 15 countries and are increasingly popular. In Belgium, where feed contaminated by dioxin was fed to livestock, 98% of beef and 56% of pork carry the Quality Line stamp. Shoppers appreciate the extra assurance.

In the USA, many food producers voluntarily label their products with country-of-origin. More have been doing so recently in reaction to consumer concerns about imported foods. Products proudly and prominently display Grown in the USA. Many on a flag sticker.

I have more to say about a *Chic & Slim* Connoisseur's approach to label information later in this chapter.

Taking Contamination Seriously

Today you must be a connoisseur of food not only to enhance your life and to keep you healthy and slim. You also must be a connoisseur to protect your life. I take the contaminated food issue very seriously. In the 1970s when I lived in India, I observed the extent to which greedy people in poorly regulated countries will go in making and selling adulterated food products in order to make a profit. In a storage box I have a fat file of newspaper and magazine clippings and observation notes I compiled on food adulteration in India. Prohibition was in force in India during those years. Often a product sold as an alcoholic beverage contained some poisonous chemical instead. I remember reading in the newspaper that more than 100 guests at a wedding reception had died from drinking something that had been sold to the host as liquor. Another common practice: unscrupulous merchants mixed iron filings in rice and other grains to make them weigh more on the scales.

The inventiveness of the adulteration was impressive. The injury and deaths caused by the contaminated products appeared to cause the perpetrators little concern. Reports today on tainted food products from China (and elsewhere) show an even greater inventiveness and absence of guilt on the part of the contaminators. Today those who would adulterate products for profit have far more sophisticated technology at their disposal than was available when I lived in India. This technology makes it easier to fake packaging and labels to disguise the contaminated products. These unscrupulous producers also have a worldwide distribution network that gives them the access to do much harm, not just in their own country, but throughout the world.

Do Our Regulations Still Protect?

Don't we have regulations in the USA that are supposed to protect us from contaminated food products?

Yes, we do have regulations. For many years those regulations protected us reasonably well. But regulations did a better job of protecting us when most of what we ate and used was grown by farmers and processed in the USA or countries with equally effective regulations. (And before the Bush administration made a concerted effort to weaken the effectiveness of the regulatory agencies.) Now, with most food being produced not by farmers but by agribusiness, and with production facilities in parts of the world where regulation is lacking, things are very different. Different and more risky.

Recently we have become aware of additional problems with regulation. A May 2007 article in the *Washington Post* discusses the difficulties in halting the imports of tainted food from China. The article quotes William Hubbard, a former associate director of the FDA, who points out that for a growing number of important food products, China has become virtually the *only* source.

China controls 80 percent of the world's production of ascorbic acid, for example, a valuable preservative that is ubiquitous in processed and other foods. Only one producer remains in the United States. This is true of many ingredients, including the wheat gluten that was initially thought to be the cause of the pet deaths. Almost none of it is made in the United States, because the Chinese sell it for less than it would cost manufacturers in the USA to make it.

The FDA and other regulatory governmental agencies served us well for many decades, but in the wake of media reports of recalls of food and other consumer products, Americans realized that we could no longer depend on governmental protections. The public demanded improvement. The Bush administration responded with a surprisingly robust plan designed to restore public confidence in product safety. *The New York Times* reported:

The proposal, prepared by an interagency panel in the wake of the recalls of food and other products made in China, provides for the federal government to revamp the way it monitors $2 trillion worth of imported products each year. Where the government has long relied on a few spot inspections at the borders, the new system would focus on catching bad products before they are exported.

The proposal would also give the Food and Drug Administration the authority to recall dangerous food products from both foreign and domestic suppliers when a company refused to do so or moved too slowly — power the agency does not have now. And it would give the F.D.A. stronger authority to demand preventive measures for high-risk foods.

We shall see if this plan becomes reality and whether sufficient funds to enforce stronger regulation will be available.

Better Protection In USA

What will be done to protect consumers from the new and very dangerous threats should be a question connoisseurs put to candidates for upcoming elections. Their answers should be on our minds when we step into the voting booths. Not only in national elections but in state and local elections as well.

I was an early financial supporter of The Center for Science in the Public Interest. With my French–influenced opinions as to fat in food, however, I later lost my enthusiasm for the group when they jumped so solidly on the all–fat–is–bad wagon. CSPI does have a useful website. Even if I still do not agree entirely with CSPI on fat, the organization is working to address problems of contamination in imported foods, as well as in those grown and processed in the USA. The bulletins CSPI posts on their website can keep you informed of problems and provide you information on how you can protect yourself.

To be *Chic & Slim* Connoisseurs of food, we need to stay *au courant*. Depending on your primary news source, the quality of product safety coverage will vary. *The New York Times* and *Washington Post* are the two newspapers I read regularly. Both have given good coverage to the food contamination topic, as have many other newspapers and radio and television networks.

Find a reliable source and check it regularly. Do not ignore a recall notice of a product you have in your house.

First Lines of Defense

I lived many years in parts of the world where food and water borne diseases are prevalent and life-threatening, and where it was necessary to be on guard constantly against contaminated foods. This experience made me a faithful follower of food safety rules. Following basic food safety rules will give you a first line of defense in case you do eat a tainted food. You will have a better chance of avoiding serious or fatal illness. The Food and Drug Administration has a food safety checkup questionnaire on their website. Answers follow the list of questions and there are instructions for scoring yourself. The prize, of course, is the security of knowing that you are keeping yourself and your family safe.

Many people violate food safety rules and do not become ill, I know. On the other hand, medical authorities estimate that many illnesses self-diagnosed as "the virus going around" are actually food poisoning from unsafe handling of food in our kitchens or in kitchens of restaurants in which we eat. Be safe. A healthy body has more chance of being slim and attractive. Chronic intestinal problems can be a real challenge to chic.

Be selective where you eat out. Choose places that you are confident are clean and that use only uncontaminated foods in preparing the dishes they serve. It's not always easy to identify the problem places. But you should try. If you do become ill and you are certain that it was food that you ate in a restaurant that caused the illness, report the matter to your local health department. This information is important for officials to do their job of protecting you.

Several years ago, a new eating place opened in town. When I mentioned to a friend who had eaten there that I planned to try the place, he advised that I order: "A hard boiled egg to go."

I got the message.

Read The Label Before You Eat

Another thing you can do to prevent buying or eating an unsafe food is read the label. Some labels are artfully deceptive, true. But usually you find *some* information. If you do not find satisfactory information, that itself may be the warning sign.

These days I am looking carefully at country-of-origin on food I buy. If I don't see Made in or Grown in (Country Name), I look for another brand that does give country of origin.

The Packed For Distribution Deception

On too many products all I am finding is the phrase "Packed For Distribution By" and then follows the name of an American company and a USA address. Unfortunately that does not tell me what I need to know: where the product was grown or processed, and by whom. Suspicious me thinks this "distribution by" labeling is a way for the company to avoid telling me the product was grown or processed in some country by someone I would prefer it was not.

Ways to Better Food

Given our problems with imported food, you admire the wisdom of the

French and of those in other countries whose government policies support and protect small farmers and food artisans. Regulations for raising livestock, growing produce, making cheeses, selling food oils give strong protections to consumers.

Quality food costs more than junk food. Americans must move beyond "low price" as the criteria for a good buy. We must become *Chic & Slim* Connoisseurs who look for the real quality in the foods we put in our shopping basket.

Foods that make us sick are not a good buy—no matter how low the price.

Choices Based On Truth

Part of being a *Chic & Slim* Connoisseur of food is demanding truthful information about food products we buy. That information should be in plain language or a prominently–displayed symbol on the product. We should not have to phone a consumer 800 number, make five menu choices and then wait on hold for two hours before some customer service representative gives us evasive answers to our questions.

A savvy connoisseur always makes choices on verifiable fact, not on advertising hype and deceptive labeling. Good health and a slim body depend on it.

Progress & Hope

Chef and food revolutionary Alice Waters' mid-1960s discovery of French food and lifestyle created in her the desire for a lifetime of good well-prepared food and civilized living. Her experience in France inspired her to promote a food revolution in the USA.

Like Alice Waters, my discovery of the joys of French food and lifestyle, lead me to use French *savoir vivre* to create for myself a rich and satisfying life wherever in the world I happened to be living. When I set out to do that, I received a fantastic bonus. I also discovered the French-inspired techniques by which I was able to solve my chief problem: how to lose the excess fat that made the first quarter century of my life so miserable.

The French-inspired techniques for slim I developed for my *Chic & Slim* system require quality food prepared and eaten in moderate quantities in a civilized manner. Even as processed and fast foods spread to even remote corners of the world, today we have a growing international organization Slow Food dedicated to promoting civilized consumption of quality food. Slow Food defines itself as a "non-profit, eco-gastronomic member-supported organization that was founded in 1989 to counteract fast food and fast life, the disappearance of local food traditions and people's dwindling interest in the food they eat, where it comes from, how it tastes and how our food choices affect the rest of the world." The movement's aims as outlined in its philosophy below are certainly in sync with our new kind of connoisseurship.

We believe that everyone has a fundamental right to pleasure and consequently the responsibility to protect the heritage of food, tradition and culture that make this pleasure possible. Our movement is founded upon this concept of eco-gastronomy—a recognition of the strong connections between plate and planet. Slow Food is good, clean and fair food. We believe that the food we eat should taste good; that it should be produced in a clean way that does not harm the environment, animal welfare or our health; and that food producers should receive fair compensation for their work.

The traditional connoisseur thinks of imported food as Beluga caviar from the Caspian or a fine Bordeaux from France. But when the *Chic & Slim* Connoisseur thinks of imported food, what more often comes to mind is fish raised in polluted ponds fed on substandard or contaminated feed, or ingredients for processed foods bought with no thought to quality from whatever area of the world the labor of exploited workers makes possible the lowest price.

The *Chic & Slim* Connoisseur thinks of imported food as food whose long distance transportation causes a loss of nutrition and taste and leaves a large carbon footprint—not to mention more possibility that it might be contaminated.

Did you realize that a recent change in regulation now allows chickens slaughtered in the USA to be shipped dead to China for processing there and then shipped back to the USA for consumption? Why you ask? Because they say it is cheaper.

For the *Chic & Slim* Connoisseur, quality food for the table is more often that which is grown close to home, in small farming operations that reward the grower with a fair share of profit for his labors. Today some regions of the USA offer more opportunity for locally grown organic produce than others. But most regions offer the possibility to produce a wide range of quality foods as we have for centuries.

While writing this section, I was clicking around on the Slow Food International website and came upon information about an Italian producer of pork who fed his animals entirely on acorns. This diet was said to produce an exquisite taste in the meat. Ah, so Italian, many Americans would think when they read about that pork producer. In fact, I had just returned from an exercise walk here in the small North Texas city in which I live. On the grounds of a large property on the edge of town, I had seen under a tall old oak, a huge porker happily munching on the acorns below. Italy, apparently, is not the only place where people fatten pigs on an exclusive diet of acorns.

From my window, I eyed the huge oak in my front yard estimating I had about a fat pig's worth of acorns strewn on the ground below. Current zoning surely would not allow it, of course. Yet behind my 83-year-old house stands the chicken house whose feathered residents many years supplied the eggs and poultry for the table here. In the small town in Oklahoma in which I grew up, until the 1970s, it was permissible for residents to keep chickens, and one cow and one calf on their property inside the city limits. Eggs and milk *chez vous*.

The pig happily munching acorns on a crisp autumn morning. The old ivy-covered red brick chicken house that sits in my back yard. My memories of delicious fruits, vegetables, dairy products and meat from the farms and gardens of my childhood testify that we can produce wonderful foods right here in the USA in almost every region. We don't need to import most of the food for everyday meals from halfway around the world.

Finding Quality Food

Given how today Americans are geared to "industrial eating," in most areas of the USA, however, the connoisseur will have to put out effort to locate quality locally produced food. Fortunately there are some wonderful Internet resources to help. *The Omnivore's Dilemma's* author Michael Pollan's website *michaelpollan.com* offers an easy-to-use set of links. One link is to *localharvest.org*. Here you type in your zip code and find listings for farms, community sustainable agriculture programs, co-ops, and farmer's markets selling locally produced food in your area. If you, like me, find little listed for your area, there are links to producers who will ship to you.

Today, most of us will not be able to supply all our food needs with locally grown organic. No more than my family was able to supply all our food needs from friends and family's farms and gardens when I was a child. Organic, for many of us, may be a matter of when we can buy it or grow it. Not daily fare. As for "locally grown" we may have to loosen our definition.

For some time, most of the zucchini for sale at my supermarket was grown in Mexico. One day, my packing box sleuthing determined the zucchini currently for sale had been grown in west Texas near Lubbock. Lubbock may be 200 miles, but Lubbock is closer than Mexico.

For years, the mushrooms I have bought at the supermarket have been grown in Watsonville, California. Watsonville is next door to Santa Cruz. The four years my son was at the university there, I thought of the Watsonville mushrooms as sort of locally grown. Not long ago, I bought, at my supermarket, mushrooms grown on a farm near Miami, Oklahoma. I was born and raised in Oklahoma and now live very near the Oklahoma Texas state line. Even though that mushroom farm is in the northeast corner of Oklahoma, I somehow think of those mushrooms as "locally grown." Oklahoma is closer than California. Oklahoma is a lot closer than China.

As a testimony on behalf of somewhat distant local, I find the Oklahoma mushrooms fresher and more flavorful than the Watsonville. While working on this section of the book, I have lunched on some delicious *omelettes aux champignons*.

However you define local, as a *Chic & Slim* Connoisseur in quest of quality food, you will be wise to seek out food produced the shortest distance away possible and support the producers, especially those from whom you can buy directly.

A *potager*, a French style kitchen garden, can also be a wonderful near source of fresh vegetables. The French have made an art of designing vegetable gardens that serve as beautiful landscaping. You can surround yourself with natural beauty that pleases the eye in addition to the palate. Most residential gardens will need some soil improvement. Raised beds that the French favor can be a quick solution to less-productive soils.

Avoid Problems, Eat Locally Grown

Shopping for locally grown offers a solution to many concerns about regulations of food import. When you buy your food from producers you know, it doesn't matter if Congress delays implementing country-of-origin labeling. You don't have to worry about deceptive labels on supermarket products or the huge percentage of imported foods the FDA was unable to inspect, or whether the Chinese will really enforce food production safety.

Buying from local producers gives you an opportunity to see the fields where and under what conditions the food you eat is produced. You can also talk with the producer about his production philosophy and methods.

When choosing quality food, *Chic & Slim* Connoisseurs also consider security of their food supply. That increasing amounts of food we eat come from the other side of the planet is troubling. Especially given the current worries about terrorism, this trend seems fraught with dangers. On the other hand, food production in small farming operations scattered across all areas of the USA is a good way to insure that no matter what wars or natural disasters occur outside or inside our borders, there will be an ample food supply.

The *Chic & Slim* Connoisseur uses quality food to be slim. That quality food can also keep us healthy and safe.

Eat quality. Be slim. Be safe.

Connoisseur Slim Today

WHAT CAN WE SAY about the food situation today for the connoisseur who wants to eat delicious, safe food and still stay slim? In comparison with five years ago when this book was first published, some things are better—and other things are looking truly depressing.

First the better. Not just in the two food stores in which I do most of my food shopping here in North Texas, but all across the USA, it is becoming easier to buy organic and locally grown food. Both my supermarkets have begun offering more locally grown produce—one even posting photographs with names and locations of area produce farmers. Both stores now offer more organic produce at reasonable prices. Especially at Walmart, the price difference between organic and produce grown with pesticides and chemical fertilizers is noticeably narrowing. If I have my choice between a pound of carrots grown with pesticides and chemicals at 78 cents and a pound of organic carrots at 98 cents, of course, I am going to buy organic.

COOL, the Country of Origin Labeling Law originally passed as part of the 2002 Farm Bill, finally went into effect in March 2009. We are seeing more food labelled with the name of country in which it was produced. Foods actually grown or manufactured in the USA are proudly displaying that information on their labels. When you encounter a product lacking a "Made In" or "Product of" on the label, there is reason to be cautious about purchasing. As before, beware the "Distributed by" and the name of a company headquartered in the USA but no indication where the food was grown or manufactured.

More good news: passage of the Food Safety Modernization Act. Incredible that before consumers pressured Congress to pass such a bill in January 2011, the Food and Drug Administration had no authority to recall contaminated products from the shelves of stores in the USA. Even if tainted food had people crowding into the emergency rooms, and even dying, the FDA could only *request* the company making the contaminated food recall it. If the company wanted to keep selling the contaminated food, it could.

Protections Against Contaminated Food

According to statistics from our Center for Disease Control, foodborne illness strikes some 48 million people in the USA annually. 128,000 of those people end up in the hospital and 3000 of them die. This Food Safety Modernization law also gives the FDA responsibility and authority for prevention efforts against contamination so people do not get sick in the first place. Throwing up and diarrhea, chief symptoms of "food poisoning," are definite challenges to your chic. Vomiting and diarrhea are not healthy ways to become slim.

By the way, just so you can better protect yourself, as an article in *The New York Times* reported recently, these days you are most likely to contact foodborne illness from leafy vegetables such as lettuce or spinach. Why from those otherwise healthy greens? Lettuce—and often spinach—are eaten raw. Their contamination usually comes via a food handler. You need to choose carefully the restaurants where you eat fresh salads. While leafy greens are the most likely source of illness, you are more likely to actually die from a foodborne illness if food contamination came via poultry. When I read that poultry statistic, I remembered those dead chickens shipped to China to be plucked I wrote about in the Slim section of the first edition of this book. I couldn't help wondering if there was any connection.

When I served in the Peace Corps in West Africa, the threat of foodborne illness was our most serious daily problem. Dysentery was more likely than poisonous snake bite. Precautions that became part of my lifestyle in those years have continued to be useful now that I again live in the USA.

The basic rule: "Don't eat anything that has not recently been through the ordeal of fire." And make sure that fire heated the food sufficiently that it killed whatever bacteria or virus it happened to be carrying. To kill *E. coli* bacteria, for instance, requires heating meat to an internal temperature of 160 degrees F. (70 degrees C.) That's hot. You need a meat thermometer to actually measure internal heat.

The website of the Centers for Disease Control and Prevention is the best resource on food safety in the USA. *www.cdc.gov/*

Gold Mine Of Information For Quality Food

As I reported in the first edition of this book, the website of food authority Michael Pollan, (author *The Omnivore's Dilemma*) is a gold mine of information for eating well and safely in the USA. The Resources section's FAQs and links are organized by category: Sustainable Eating & Nutrition, Growing Food, Politics & Policy, Animal Welfare, Journalism & Writing, and For Parents & Kids. If you are not already familiar with this website, you may find useful information there. *michaelpollan.com/resources/*

Michael Pollan's answer to one frequently asked question about soy caught my attention. When the concerns about side effects of taking hormone replacement therapy caused doctors to begin discouraging women from the therapy, many doctors began urging women to eat more soy for the phytoestrogens available in soy products. According to Michael Pollan, eating non-traditional versions of soy may not be a good idea. Michael Pollan writes:

> "But today we're eating soy in ways Asian cultures with a much longer experience of the plant would not recognize: "Soy protein isolate," "soy isoflavones," "textured vegetable protein" from soy and soy oils (which now account for a fifth of the calories in the American diet) are finding their way into thousands of processed foods, with the result that Americans now eat more soy than the Japanese or the Chinese do."

Much of the soy available in the USA is from genetically modified soybeans. For some of us, that is an additional concern.

In 2000, when I wrote the recipe section of the first edition of *Chic &*
Slim Encore, because of that advice to certain age women to eat more soy,
I was including soy in a number of forms into my diet. In recent years
however, not so much. I never really transitioned from dairy to soy milk. (I
think soy milk tastes ghastly in my breakfast tea.) I haven't used soy flour in
my baking in a couple of years. I probably have not included TVP, textured
vegetable (soy) protein, in my cauliflower curry or vegetable stir-fry more
than twice in the past year. Soy products, other than tofu, just don't agree
with my digestive system. Reading Michael Pollan's comments on soy, I
decided perhaps my neglect of soy may have not been a bad thing.

Raging Battle Over GMO Labeling

While the situation for buying quality food has been steadily improving,
currently a battle rages over the labeling of genetically modified or
genetically engineered foods, GMOs. Also known as Frankenfoods.

In the autumn of 2012, Monsanto, producer of herbicides, pesticides
and genetically modified seeds—along with other usual suspects DuPont,
Pepsico, Kraft, Coca-Cola and Nestle—spent over $40 million to defeat
a California proposition that would have required foods that contained
genetically modified organisms GMOs to indicate so on the label. This
was not any attempt to actually ban GMOs, as is the case in a number of
other countries. (Even Egypt, a poor country in political turmoil, bans the
importation of GMO foods.) With the California law, consumers simply
wanted, as in Europe where labeling is required, to know whether foods did
or did not contain GMOs. The issue is "right to know."

You can consider this issue from several angles. One perspective is that
currently, according to the Dept. of Agriculture, 93% of soybeans, 90%
canola and 88% corn raised in the USA are genetically modified. Because
of their widespread use, GMOs are in virtually every food you find in your
supermarket. Even foods labeled organic are allowed up to 5% GMOs.
(Learning that fact startled and disturbed me.) Many foods that contain
no GMOs are already displaying NO GMO labels because the companies
that produce them know that many consumers prefer foods that have not

been messed with in a laboratory. So instead of a law requiring labeling, consumers could just reasonably assume that if a food does not carry a NO GMO label, at least some of its ingredients have been genetically modified.

One interesting recent development in the GMO labeling war is that some media are reporting that Walmart might favor GMO labeling. Walmart as the largest grocery seller in the USA already exercises great clout in demanding companies to meet Walmart's particular packaging demands. If Walmart began to demand GMO labels, it might not make as much difference whether various states pass GMO labeling laws. The FDA recognizes no problem with GMOs, so there is little hope for a national labeling requirement.

The extreme difficulty people in the USA face in avoiding foods with GMOs and other problems associated with raising crops from genetically engineered seeds is one cause for depression about food in the USA. And, of course, there is our ever worsening problem with excess weight and obesity and their related health problems.

Do GMOs Facilitate Weight Gain?

Is there any indication that eating genetically modified foods makes it more difficult to stay slim? One doctor whose experience indicates that the answer is yes, at least for one genetically modified grain, is William Davis, M.D. He is author of the popular books *Wheat Belly* and *Wheat Belly Cookbook*. Dr. Davis writes:

> I believe that the increased consumption of grains—or more accurately, the increased consumption of this genetically altered thing called modern wheat—explains the contrast between slender, sedentary people of the fifties and overweight twenty-first-century people, triathletes included. I recognize that declaring wheat a malicious food is like declaring that Ronald Reagan was a Communist. It may seem absurd, even unpatriotic, to demote an iconic dietary staple to the status of public health hazard. But I will make the case that the world's most popular grain is also the world's most destructive dietary ingredient.

Back in the late 1990s and early 2000s—long before Dr. Davis and his theories came to public attention—I had a positive experience eliminating wheat from my diet. I wrote about this experience on the *Chic & Slim* website. What prompted me to eliminate wheat was the information from several sources that wheat slowed metabolism. Eliminating wheat would help my body burn more calories, a wonderful aid to weight control, I decided. I was also seeking relief from a painful digestive problem. Substituting other grains, particularly buckwheat and amaranth for wheat was recommended in Peter J. D'Adamo's book *Eat Right for Your Type*. A friend whose family health history I knew well had a good experience with the D'Adamo program and recommended it. By that time, I was so tired of my digestive problem that none of the medical doctors I consulted had been able to help, that I was ready to try any reasonable program.

I never achieved total wheatlessness. (And I certainly did not eliminate gluten) But for a year or so I eliminated about 90% of the amount of wheat I had previously eaten on a daily basis. I converted my Barone Breakfast Bread to a wheatless version using rye, oats, corn, spelt, rice and buckwheat flours. During that time of dramatically reduced wheat consumption, my severe digestive problem improved dramatically, seven pounds melted away (my wrists got really bony and I had the slimmest thighs of my life), and I sustained a noticeable increase in energy.

Slowly I began re-incorporating more wheat into my diet. I've put on a few pounds—but still fit into my benchmark jeans. My digestive problems flare up from time to time. Still I try to keep wheat at a minimum because the less wheat I eat, the easier it is to stay slim and the better I feel. (Assuming other factors remain equal.) I incorporate much buckwheat (organic), rye (organic), millet, rice and oats into my diet. I also rarely buy commercially baked bread. Though I do buy some cookies, all of these *petit gâteau sec* made in Europe or the UK with the exception of Newman's Own Fig Newmans.

Is Giving Up Wheat And/Or Gluten Worth It?

A recent all-wheat bread experience may be instructive. When I was working very hard on the e-book conversions of three *Chic & Slim* books, I decided to save the time I spent on bread baking by buying good quality commercial breads. Grains breads, though expensive, were acceptable substitutes. But one day I was enticed by a lovely all-natural (flour, water, salt, and yeast) Tuscan-style *boule*. All white flour. No whole grains. Oh, dear! Eating the usual amount for breakfast, an hour later I was starving. My digestive system began sending out protests. Though it was only eight o'clock in the morning, I felt sleepy. Enough of this, I said. I would have to find something besides bread baking to eliminate to have more time for my writing.

In the certain age book, *Chic & Slim Toujours*, I write that, during my successful weight loss using French techniques, my breakfast was a chunk of (unbleached wheat flour) baguette with butter and French jam with a cup of French roast coffee. I further report that type of breakfast will no longer see me through to lunch. I surmised it was because of changes in my body due to age. Now, as I read about positive health improvements people are experiencing today eliminating wheat and/or gluten from their diets, I wonder if today, if I breakfasted on a chunk of baguette made with the same French flour as in those 1960s baguettes, would that provide me a satisfying breakfast equal to what I derive from a piece of my homemade breakfast bread that is at least half oats or corn or rye?

No denying that some Americans are seeing weight loss and health improvements from eliminating wheat and/or gluten from their diets. Questions arise. Is it the elimination of wheat and gluten that is solely responsible for the positive results? Or do some benefits come from the more nutritious (and less genetically modified) grains that replace wheat? Most Americans get the largest part of their wheat and gluten intake from commercial breads and pastries that contain many chemicals and highly processed substances as well as liberal amounts of salt and sugar. When someone eliminates wheat, they also eliminate those unhealthy elements. Does this additional elimination substantially contribute to the weight loss and improved health?

A further question presents itself: If we could go back to the less modified and less processed and chemically adulterated foods, the kind were available from any grocery store in the USA in the 1950s (and before), would we go back to lower levels of excess weight and obesity that we had in those days? Would we see a smaller percentage of the population suffering diabetes and other diet and lifestyle-related health problems?

The answer to that question based on the latest medical research is a resounding yes.

Connoisseurship For Quality Food

Given the food industry's successful defeat of California's GMO labeling proposition and considering the stranglehold American agribusiness and related industries have on our Congress and Food and Drug Administration, it seems highly unlikely that we shall ever go back to the quality of food that was commonly available in those earlier, better times in the USA. If we want to enjoy healthy food and stay slim, we must become connoisseurs of quality food. Like a connoisseur of fine art or fine wine, we must dedicate money and effort to acquiring quality food.

Or relocate to a country where laws and regulations make quality food more easily available.

Connoisseur Safe

STAYING SAFE. The plot of *How To Steal A Million* revolves around Nicole Bonnet's efforts to keep her father safe. And keep herself safe as well. When discovery of his art forgeries appears imminent, Charles Bonnet tells his daughter that she must go to America or the Orient. *Horreurs!*

For this chic Parisienne who was born and has lived her whole life in Paris, such exile is too terrible to contemplate. (Such a long way from Givenchy!) So Nicole sets out to keep her father safe from prison and herself in Paris. She realizes that she cannot accomplish this feat alone.

Connoisseurship can make us safer. Making quality the standard for everything in our lives will be one of the best things we can do to protect ourselves and our families. But we cannot always act alone. Sometimes government (local, state or federal) must play a role. When it does, we must insist that government plays its role well.

If we find the various threats to our lives growing, a root cause is that in recent past elections too many Americans rejected quality leadership. In the anti-quality environment of the USA, too many Americans preferred to vote for a candidate with whom they felt comfortable rather than one of intelligence, character and ability. Late 1990s and early 21st century, US presidents were chosen by an electorate who put too much emphasis on likeability. As a result, in neither presidency did we receive the quality leadership we might have had electing other candidates. Making a choice on likeability is self-defeating. If you had a brain tumor, would you choose your neurosurgeon on the basis of someone fun to go to lunch with?

Connoisseurs of Conservation

Hydrogen cells. Solar panels. Electric cars. Wind farms. Ethanol. All these ideas for new energy sources to combat global warming are being proposed. But there is an easier, cheaper, more immediate way to deal with the problems of carbon emissions and climate change. This way can aid us in staying chic, slim, safe and rich. How? We can become connoisseurs of conservation. Anyone who has lived outside the USA and seen how much more frugal people in other nations are about energy consumption, knows Americans are champion wasters. The good news about rampant American wasting is: conservation could make huge savings in energy and resources.

A couple of years ago when the price of gas shot up to never before highs, I observed one major difference from the reaction to the energy crisis in the mid-1970s. When the price of energy rose 30 years previously, the media bombarded us with suggestions for conserving energy. Some ideas were more practical than others. I remember an article in a women's magazine that admonished homemakers to plan their menus so it would only be necessary to open the freezer door once every two weeks. Try it.

Recently when the price of filling the tank of an SUV approached the cost of buying a kitchen appliance, the loudest calls were for exotic and yet-to-be-perfected technologies. These drowned out voices saying things we can do right now: Turn off the television when you aren't in the room, energy efficient light bulbs, put on a sexy sweater and turn down the thermostat in cold weather, vacation close to home instead of driving across country. Stop buying bottled water from distant places and use a home water filter. A full list of easy-to-make energy-saving changes would fill pages.

In a 2007 article, *New York Times* columnist Nicholas Kristof quoted everyone from Peter Robertson, vice chairman of Chevron to Diana Farrell of McKinsey Global Institute, to James Woolsey, energy expert and former director of the CIA, that conservation is the best and most immediate way to fight global warming and cut our dependence on foreign oil. In his blog comments Nicholas Kristof added: "There's also a major national security argument for conservation: The more we reduce our oil dependency, the less vulnerable we are to the whims of Iran and Venezuela. What's more, if we curb demand, that tends to dampen the oil price—which means less revenue for Iran to invest in nuclear weapons."

For our safety, we should become connoisseurs of the best methods of energy conservation. We should take as much pride in a new energy efficient refrigerator as in a new designer dress. We should consider a fuel efficient vehicle as beneficial to our children's future health as regular dental checkups.

Individual efforts, of course, cannot solve this enormous problem. We must elect to public office those who champion conservation and national energy independence. We should make sure that useful legislation is passed. Sooner rather than later.

Quality Against Flu

Does your family have a flu pandemic emergency plan?

What? you say. You couldn't even locate the camping lantern in the garage the last time the electrical power went out.

How concerned should we be about a possible flu pandemic? As for any possible national emergency, we must give thought to what action we will take if it becomes necessary. As for any epidemic, the CDC website is the best source of information about plans and preparations for a possible flu pandemic. Call your local government information number to inquire about a community flu pandemic plan. Don't be surprised if there is none.

Flu comes in seasons, but MRSA, or methicillin-resistant *Staphylococcus aureus*, is an antibiotic resistant staph infection currently responsible for more deaths annually in the USA than AIDS. Life-threatening and also chic-threatening because MRSA is one of the "flesh-eating" staph infections. Further bad news about MRSA is that according to a report on a study published in *The Journal of the American Medical Association,* 85 percent of cases are acquired through health-care treatment.

What is the best preventative for MRSA? Experts recommend frequent hand washing, also one of the best protections against the common cold. Prompt attention to cuts and scratches are advised.

Quality To Protect Against Tainted Products

When media reports appeared that dogs and cats were dying from tainted pet food, Americans were shocked and dismayed. When the reports continued: tainted toothpaste and cough syrup, counterfeit glucose test strips that gave faulty readings, millions of children's toys and baby bibs because they contained dangerous levels of lead, the shock and dismay deepened.

Like many Americans, I was aware and vigilant against the threat of terrorist attacks and pandemic flu and the perils of global warming. But until the puppy dogs and kitty cats began to die and the pet food recall notices went out, I had little idea how vulnerable we had become to unsafe consumer products. I believed that our consumer laws and regulatory agencies protected us.

Why hadn't we been more aware of what was really happening? Why were we not more aware that substandard products made in parts of the world where product safety regulations could be ignored were sitting on the shelves of stores all across the USA?

If Americans in the early 21st century felt overly secure about product safety, there were good reasons. For the past century, our federal and state regulations and agencies have protected us reasonably well. A magazine cartoon that sticks vividly in my memory was one in (I think) *The Saturday Evening Post*. An ordinary suburban house is surrounded by an army tank and a team of commandos have automatic weapons pointed at the front door. A federal agent in a trench coat standing on the front steps is saying to a rotund middle-aged man in the doorway: "Mr. Smith, we have a report that you took that little white tag off your mattress."

Some people thought our regulations overprotected us.

As for the threats that we came to see more clearly in 2007, in hindsight, it seems that most of the books and articles about intellectual piracy and counterfeit products focused on luxury goods, pirated CDs and DVDs, computer software, films and music. Big corporations were losing profit. But those knockoffs and illegal copies weren't perceived as a danger to individuals. Our guilt level was kept low because the big corporations weren't being hurt that badly. If the man in the jeans and dirty T-shirt was selling $20 "Louie Vuitton" bags at the flea market, Louis Vuitton was doing quite well selling the real bags in Paris.

So what if Microsoft was losing millions from the sale of counterfeit copies of Windows? No one was worrying that the little Gates children would have to go through the winter without shoes.

But people and organizations were trying to warn us about the problems.

Not long after it was published, my son passed along his copy of *Illicit: How Smugglers, Traffickers, and Copycats Are Hijacking the Global Economy* by Moisés Naím, editor and publisher of *Foreign Policy*. About the same time I read Thomas Friedman's *The World is Flat: A Brief History of the Twenty-first Century*. I remember a comment that *The World is Flat* was the positive of globalization and *Illicit* was the negative.

The World is Flat was still on the bestseller lists when I wrote this in August 2007, *Illicit* is listed at 11,570 on the *Amazon.com* bestselling. Who says we aren't optimists? Perhaps if Moisés Naím were the Master of Metaphor that Thomas Friedman is, or if anyone could spell, much less pronounce, his name, his message might have been read by more Americans. His 2005 book is full of warnings about the dangers from the booming illegal side of the global economy. He explains the increase in counterfeit goods:

> Once, counterfeits traded across borders were highly concentrated in the fashion industry and focused on luxury goods: Pierre Cardin shirts, Gucci handbags, Louis Vuitton luggage, and the like. These remain popular rip-off targets, of course, but so too now are industrial bolts, cigarettes, DVDs, detergent, garbage bags, video games, shock absorbers, asthma inhalers, marine gauges, cigars, and champagne . . . . factories in Mexico purchase raw materials from India with which they formulate and package fake medicine, its active ingredient watered down or simply absent, which they sell to Americans in Tijuana or on the Internet . . . . More worrisome still is the spread of fake aircraft parts.

Another who tried to warn us was Maria Livanos Cattaui, Secretary General of the International Chamber of Commerce. In a 2005 op-ed for the *International Herald Tribune* she wrote that counterfeiting and intellectual piracy had become as serious a threat as theft of personal property. That threat was increasing because product counterfeiting and intellectual piracy was more profitable than smuggling and selling narcotics but carried much less risk for those who engaged in it.

The Secretary General further warned that "perpetrators do not pay tax, do not respect labor laws and do not care about product quality or safety . . . . consumers are subject to risks to health and safety when products such as toys, medicines, foodstuffs, beverages, airplane parts or car parts are reproduced without the safety features of the originals."

We have seen all too clearly how those missing safety features are causing serious problems today.

In 2005 *Business Week* magazine sounded warnings about out of control intellectual piracy and counterfeiting. Their cover story on 7 February 2005 had a one word title: Fakes! The message: Counterfeiting had gone from a local nuisance to a global threat. China was responsible for about two-thirds of those counterfeit products sold around the world. Unscrupulous wholesalers fob off fakes on small auto-repair shops, office-supply stores, or independent pharmacies by saying they have bargain-priced—but not suspiciously cheap—oil filters, printer cartridges, or bottles of shampoo that another retailer returned, or which are close to their sell-by date. Some traders mix phonies in with authentic goods. "It's easy to slide a stack of fake Levis under the real ones," says one investigator based in Shanghai. "Most inspectors and buyers can't tell the difference."

Some of those fake products are dangerous. Swiss pharmaceutical company Novartis determined counterfeiters used yellow highway paint to achieve the right color match for fakes of one of its painkillers. Yet nothing in *Illicit* or media stories on counterfeit products made me suspect that thousands of dogs and cats would sicken and some die because of contaminated wheat gluten.

When I read the media report of the pet food recall, my first thought was that the French were wise to prepare pet foods in the family kitchen. I had written on the *Chic & Slim* website about this and given readers a link to an article that mentioned the recipe for dog food that French actress Brigitte Bardot had prepared for her dogs. It was the basic recipe I had been given: rice, vegetables (zucchini or green beans and carrots) and meat.

But why on earth were American pet food companies importing wheat gluten? The USA is a major wheat growing country. The answer: because Chinese wheat gluten is the cheapest.

Old Rules Need Updating

As I followed revelations of how the pet food had become contaminated, it became clear that two tenets of careful consumerism I had followed all my adult life no longer applied in this era of globalization. Read the label, we were told. But on a counterfeit product the label is a copy of the one on the real product. It does not warn you of a dangerous ingredient, or a contaminated ingredient, or a missing ingredient.

A second tenet that no longer applies is that buying name brands gives assurance of a safe product. Many recalled pet foods were well-known brands that certainly were not cheap.

As Americans learned about pet food problems, it occurred to many that wheat gluten might not be the only contaminated product imported into the USA from China. Products humans were swallowing or rubbing on might pose dangers.

Counterfeit Cosmetics

As I researched counterfeit consumer products, cosmetics made almost every list of fakes. Chic women worldwide buy and use makeup and skin care products to enhance their appearance. Counterfeit cosmetics are finding their way into distribution systems. Where are those fakes being sold? Do counterfeit cosmetics pose a possible danger to those of us who might inadvertently purchase them?

In a *New York Times* article by Sabra Chartrand, she explained: Black market employs thousands of workers and represents a significant portion of the economy. Illicit manufacturers operate factories all over China, where the knockoffs are produced for a fraction of the price of brand-name goods, and are so cleverly packaged that it is hard to tell them from the real products.

Not all counterfeits stay in China. Fake goods are shipped all over the world. It's difficult for distributors in recipient countries to tell they have received counterfeit products.

Moisés Naím in his book *Illicit* explains: Another reason for the boom in counterfeits is that the facilities and equipment their manufacture requires have spread around the world—not least thanks to the original manufacturers themselves who have shared technology and know-how to penetrate new markets. Many items we think of as luxuries—high-end cosmetics, for instance, or fancy designer apparel—are made to the brand owner's specifications by mass-production factories that work for multiple clients.

One factory might make cosmetic products for several different brands, each to the recipe of that particular brand. It might make LuxuryBrand facial toner and also DirtCheap facial toner, but each would be made to its own recipe.

Apparently what often happens is that a factory will make and bottle the products for the LuxuryBrand company and ship those off to the distributors. Then they turn around and illegally make and bottle the same products in identical packing and labels. Bottles and labels are the same for the real and the counterfeit product, but the counterfeit version may not contain the same listed ingredients in the listed amounts. Substandard ingredients might be used. Some ingredients might be missing.

For example, in a hydroquinone-based skin bleaching cream, the counterfeit version would contain the same inactive ingredients as the real version, but only minimal hydroquinone. Perhaps none. In the scariest scenario, a dangerous chemical might be substituted for hydroquinone.

With fake cosmetics the counterfeiters always have cover if they get the packaging and labels right and the product looks authentic. Since no cosmetic product is effective for everyone, if someone did not get satisfactory results, they would think the product just didn't work for them. Or that their body had developed resistance to the active ingredient, as happens often. Or they were allergic.

A counterfeit cosmetic with minimal or no active ingredient would waste your money and fail to achieve the results you desire. A counterfeit containing a dangerous substitute ingredient could cause problems. Serious problems. Perhaps on your face.

The good news is that while billions of dollars of counterfeit cosmetics are sold every year, in my research, I did not find media reports of serious health problems linked to fakes. But a 7 December 2007 report in *The New York Times* on China's crackdown on producers of unsafe food contained the statement: "Hong Kong food safety experts say they are also investigating cosmetics that may contain toxic substances." We should be cautious about where we purchase cosmetics, especially those sold by online merchants.

The Toy Story

Summer 2007 when the toy companies began recalling toys because of lead contamination problems, I was shocked.

I believed lead paint on toys sold by American toy companies was a thing of the past. When my son was a child in the 1970s, when I purchased a toy made by Fisher-Price or Mattel or other well-known American toy company, I did so with a feeling of security that those companies would not market a toy with any paint containing lead. I also felt secure that toys marketed by respected major American toy companies would not contain parts small enough to be swallowed. When the recall notices for lead paint and small parts went out, I was shocked.

In August 2007 when Mattel recalled 967,000 Fisher-Price toys in the USA because of lead paint, I was even more shocked. Fisher-Price! True, many parents have vivid memories of the unexpected agony of stepping barefoot in the dark on one of those Fisher-Price Little People. Even under the impact of daddy's full weight, those little critters never crumbled.

So the idea that a Fisher-Price toy might be defective was shocking.

More shocks came a few weeks later when there were more recalls by American toy manufacturers because of lead paint and parts that could be swallowed. The unsettling news was the information that the small parts were not some unauthorized substitution done by the Chinese manufacturer. The magnets had been in the design submitted to them by the American company.

Wasn't there anyone at the toy company charged with looking over a design sketch or a sample product to check for something as basic as a small part that can be broken off or otherwise detached?

Anyone in the business of making and selling toys for children should know if there is any part of the toy that can be detached, there will be children who will detach it. Once detached, their first and immediate action will be to put it into their little mouths. And if Mommy tries to remove the item from their little mouths, their first and immediate reaction will be to defy Mommy by swallowing the detached part.

Why were these toys in stores before serious problems were discovered? Why weren't representatives of these American toy companies overseeing the manufacture of the products sold under their labels? In any case, wasn't the Consumer Products Safety Commission, that federal agency set up to protect Americans from injuries from faulty or dangerous products, supposed to make sure these items are intercepted before they reach the consumer? In any case, they did not.

Obviously our government regulations and enforcement agencies need updating. They need more personnel and funding. Yet we cannot depend on government to do it all. Experts who study the situation assure us that it is going to take strong efforts by a variety of entities.

Profit is the counterfeiters' motive. Nations must cooperate with businesses, individuals and non-governmental organizations to make illegal distribution of counterfeit and contaminated products unprofitable. Stop profits and you stop counterfeiting.

Provenance: Connoisseur Safety Tool

Better regulations and enforcement will help. Yet we need a way by which consumers can identify safe and effective products. For this, we new-style connoisseurs must borrow a tool from traditional connoisseurship: Provenance.

When an art connoisseur considers purchasing an expensive work of art, they first insist on knowing the provenance. Provenance is a trustworthy, documented history of the work from its creation to its present ownership. Provenance tells the connoisseur several important things: Who created the work and where. All the times it has changed hands, who the subsequent owners were, where they kept the work of art, any cleaning or restoration done. Gaps in the provenance alert a prospective buyer to possible problems.

As I worked on this book section, I spent time examining labels of consumer products that I use on a regular basis. On the T.N. Dickinson's witch hazel I use on my skin, the words "MADE IN THE U.S.A." all in capital letters no less, was reassuring. But on products such as the multipurpose disinfecting solution that I use for my contact lenses the address of the corporate headquarters is no longer enough in an era when American companies contract the manufacture of their products outside the USA. I use that product on lenses that go onto my eyes. I have to know that this solution will adequately disinfect my lenses. I need to be sure that there is no contamination with dangerous chemicals. I need to know that this product is actually the one by the company shown on the label, not a counterfeit product that was substituted into the distribution system at some point.

It is time that we know the provenance of all potentially harmful products. We need to know who manufactured the product and the street address in what city in what country the plant was located. Exact location is important, especially for any product made in China. Investigations have reported addresses given for some Chinese companies find empty buildings. The work has been subcontracted to other producers, many of these located in areas known for counterfeiting and substandard products. Any part of the manufacturing process in such an area would be a tip-off to problems.

American companies could easily provide consumers with the provenance of their products. Almost every American and major global company has a website. It would be easy for them to post the provenance of a product by identifying it by lot number. If a product, such as my contact lens disinfecting solution, contains ingredients that have registered trademarks, the provenance would include the name of the company and location of the plant of each of those trademarked products.

The provenance of a product should also include its chain of distribution. Counterfeits are often slipped into the distribution systems by a wholesale distributor. When I buy a bottle of contact lens disinfecting solution at my local drugstore, I want to know the channel this product traveled from the manufacturer to sales outlet. If the address of a wholesaler in the distribution chain sounds fictitious or is not available, I would have reason to believe something might be wrong with the product.

Just as technology exists to create an indistinguishable-from-the real package that contains a counterfeited, substandard product, technology exists that can help us document and make easily available to consumers a trustworthy and documented provenance that will assure us of buying a product of real quality.

Forbes online posted a 9 August 2007 AP story by Barbara Ortutay that IBM had launched an ePedigree technology that uses radio-frequency identification, or RFID tags, to create electronic certificates of authenticity for medications, down to the individual bottle as they move from manufacturers and distributors to pharmacies and hospitals.

While these RFID tags would probably not discourage all counterfeiting, they would enable concerned consumers to make sure the medication they purchased was not counterfeit.

For children's toys, RFID tags (can these be swallowed?) might be overkill. Yet the tags might reassure concerned parents if they could go to a toy company's website and determine who and where in the world was making their children's playthings.

In a September 2007 *New York Times* article, Eric Lipton reported

Senate hearings into how children's toys could be made safer. He quoted Jerry Storch, chairman of Toys "R" Us, the leading toy retailer in the USA, who suggested printing a code onto toys so parents can more easily identify a recalled product.

That same code could serve as the identifier to which the complete provenance of a toy could be linked.

People Provenance

Provenance is useful not only for consumer products. Likewise, in an age when people no longer are born, live and die in the same geographic location and know all their neighbors, learning the provenance of individuals with whom we develop business or personal relationships is also important. Like products on the store shelves, individuals may not be what they seem at first glance. Here, too, knowing the provenance can protect us.

Several years ago, a young woman of my acquaintance, a middle school teacher, was shocked to learn that the man she had married some months before had previously been in prison for *murdering his first wife.* Checking the man's provenance in early stages of their relationship would have prevented the shock, and the subsequent divorce that she and her family felt a necessary precaution.

Proven Value of Provenance

For centuries provenance has been an effective tool for traditional connoisseurs in authenticating art. Today, we have the technology and the infrastructure to make provenance an effective tool to protect *Chic & Slim* Connoisseurs from dangerous consumer products. We must demand it. Let companies know we will not buy potentially harmful products unless they give us truthful information about who made the product and where they manufactured or processed it .

Our lives, or the life of someone we love, could depend on it.

PROVENANCE

Ignore It at Your Peril

— Forbes

~

Connoisseur Safe Today

SURELY THERE HAD BEEN problems somewhere. At the time I was writing the Safe section in the first edition of this *Connoisseur* book, knowing how counterfeit cosmetics were produced, I was surprised serious problems with these counterfeits had not been reported. But search as I did, I found no reports. In the ensuing five years there have been many reports of problems with counterfeit cosmetics. Serious problems. Let me tell you about some so you can better protect yourself.

A counterfeit cosmetic with minimal or no active ingredient would waste your money and fail to achieve the results you desire. But a counterfeit cosmetic containing a dangerous substitute or additional ingredient could cause serious problems. On your face. And that is exactly what has been happening.

According to an article in *The New York Times* in January 2010, some of the counterfeit versions of hydroquinone skin lightening creams have been found to contain a powerful steroid clobetasol propionate. Product guidelines for physicians who would prescribe a medication containing this ingredient state definitely clobetasol propionate should not be used on the face—nor elsewhere on the body for a maximum time of two consecutive weeks. But many women have been using those skin-lightening creams containing clobetasol propionate on their faces—for years.

Women who bought skin lightening creams at beauty shops, beauty supply stores or online have been driven to seek treatment from dermatologists offices and hospitals when their problems with these creams became severe. Given the length some women used these creams, it was not surprising they developed problems with facial skin so thin that it bruised at a touch, visible capillaries and stubborn acne. Those topical steroids found in lightening creams in some cases caused high blood pressure, elevated blood sugar, or stretch marks that remained permanent. Mercury, a poison that can damage the nervous system, has also been found in some counterfeit hydroquinone skin-lightening creams.

The possibility of buying a counterfeit cosmetic that will do you harm is the best reason to avoid buying a "to be prescribed by a doctor only" skin product sold without a doctor's prescription. Do not trust their labels. Harmful ingredients in counterfeit cosmetics are unlikely to be listed on the label. Also in the skin lightening product from France sold as Fair & White, the over-the-counter version has 1.9 % hydroquinone, legal to be sold without prescription. But counterfeit versions of Fair & While have been found in testing to contain 4% to 5% hydroquinone, amounts that legally require a doctor's prescription in the USA. For women of color, a serious problem from the misuse of hydroquinone is a blue-black darkening of the skin—a problem doctors report they are seeing more frequently.

Whatever cosmetic products we use, it is vital that we only use those that will correct skin problems and make us more attractive—not ones that cause us more disfiguring problems than we had before the treatment.

Problems have been so great that hydroquinone skin products are now banned in Europe, I understand. But products containing this skin lightener are still in wide use in the USA. The aesthetician who did my microdermabrasion encouraged me to buy Obagi Clear with 4% hydroquinone. I did buy. Then she became annoyed when, for two months, I refused to open the package. I had reservations about hydroquinone. She argued that she and many of her clients had used Obagi Clear without problems. She had even met Dr. Obagi at a training conference, and he had tested the product on himself and his skin was wonderful. (Whether or not this later was true, I am not absolutely sure. But Obagi is a respected brand used enthusiastically by many women.)

I did relent and used the 4% hydroquinone Obagi without problems and did see some lightening of dark spots. But by the time that 4% percent hydroquinone was finished, I had decided 4% was stronger than I felt comfortable using, I switched to Paula's Choice Clearly Remarkable 2% hydroquinone with BHA and actually got better skin lightening results on age spots, mole color and facial scars than I did with the twice as strong Obagi product. And the Paula's Choice was more economical.

Smartphones And Tablet Computers Under Attack

When I published the first edition of this book, smartphones were still very new. Tablet computers existed in some early incarnations, but the iPad, Kindle Fire and Nexus tablets were still some years away. Now there are hundreds of millions of smartphones and tablet computers in use. These marvelous devices bring us entertainment and assistance with our life and work. But like personal computers, the Internet, and email, these devices attract vandals and criminals who want to exploit these devices for their own evil aims. Security experts predict that we will see a momentous increase this year in malware targeting smartphones and tablet computers. Devices that run on the Android system are felt to be particularly vulnerable.

Those of us who favor devices on Apple's iOS cannot be complacent. But as long as the iOS device has not been "jailbroken," there seems to be minimal vulnerability. (Jailbreaking is using a software or hardware exploit so that the user can download applications, extensions, or themes not available through the official Apple App Store)

For those on Android systems, there are steps you can take to protect yourself from the malware threat. Online articles and bulletins from the FBI list those steps. Marguerite Reardon who writes CNET's Ask Maggie column sums up the basics:

Install security apps on your device that scan for malware, track lost devices, backs-up data, and remotely wipes lost handsets.

Download apps only from trusted and legitimate app stores and app developers.

Encrypt data stored on your device.

Decline to download apps that access and share your personal information, such as location or contacts.

On this last point, the writer points out that you should be concerned about protecting your private information. "While there's no question that key-loggers can gain access to your sensitive data, there are also legitimate applications that track your GPS location, automatically tag photos with timestamps and geolocation information, and read your contacts. These apps may not be malware per se, but they compromise your privacy and there is always a risk that the information gathered could be misused." Stalking, identity theft, anyone?

The FBI advises that your first line of defense is to understand how the device you are using works. To my horror over the years, I have found a surprising number of women who have used personal computers and computerized devices for decades but have never taken the time to learn how these devices work beyond the bare minimum that they do with them. Nor do these women understand how to set up the devices for secure use. As a consequence, they often are unable to take advantage of features that would make their work more efficient and their lives more pleasurable. They can't troubleshoot problems, and can't answer basic questions about their device when someone knowledgeable offers to help them. They leave themselves—and unfortunately others—vulnerable.

No one would call me a techie. I have to put out effort to understand computers and computerized devices. So when I buy a new computer, or iPod or tablet computer, before I put the device in operation, I read the user guide. I also read online articles about the product. I familiarize myself with the software that I will be using with the device. I set aside a "learning time" that saves a lot of time in the long run. I invest in books that will help if I run into problems. David Pogue's *Missing Manuals* are always useful. The original *Chic & Slim* website was designed with the mouse in one hand and Elizabeth Castro's *HTML Visual Quickstart Guide* in the other. Impossible to have done the job without Liz. I devote a hour of so a week to updating my understanding of Internet and computer security. The cybercriminals are always one of two steps ahead of us. We cannot afford to slip behind.

As columnist Maureen Dowd wrote in *The New York Times*:

We are so dizzy and intoxicated by our new toys — from iPhones to drones — that we are hopelessly addicted to them before we fully understand the downsides.

The instant gratification they offer makes us shortsighted in an unprecedented way. It's insane how vulnerable we've made ourselves, like drunks failing to look around as they walk into traffic. Hackers could shut down the way we live, and if they hacked into drones or nuclear codes, determine the way we die. If you think it through, which most of us avoid, the prospect of Techmaggedon is terrifying.

Safety From That Dangerous Stuff

In the first edition of this book, I recounted all the product problems consumers were having, not with only with counterfeit items, but serious problems with products from major American manufacturing companies. The problems with toys were particularly disturbing. 2007, the year I was writing the book, has now come to be called the "Year of the Recall." In the USA that year the Consumer Product Safety Commission issued a record-breaking 473 product recalls. Consumers were outraged with all the problems, especially when they learned that many of the problems stemmed, not from the Chinese manufacture of these products, but from the design by the American company. As a result we got the Consumer Product Safety Improvement Act passed in 2008. The act increases funding and adds new staff devoted to consumer product safety. The act aims at prevention of problems rather than recalls after damage has been done. We have a long way to go in this area. In the meantime, the CPSC has an excellent Recalls section of their website. If you are concerned that any products you own or are using might possibly start a fire, explode in your face, damage your skin, sicken your toddler, or strangle your dog, this is the place to find that information.

People Provenance

In the first edition of this book, I advocated people provenance, a thorough checking into the life history of someone with whom you might establish a business or personal relationship. Checking information about a person on the Internet is now standard practice.

While I am not a fan of Facebook, and I do not have a Facebook page, I will acknowledge that one aim of The Hoodied One and his cohorts in creating Facebook was to allow users to evaluate people with whom they were considering having a relationship.

The question then arises as to whether, in the case of the example I gave in the first edition of this book, the man in question would have put on his Facebook page that he had been in prison for murdering his first wife. Probably not. On the other hand, there might be other clues, for instance, a period of time for which there was no accounting. Or maybe not.

Facebook does not permit those incarcerated a Facebook page, though many inmates have smuggled cellphones with which they can keep their Facebook pages updated. Some have a person on the outside update their Facebook page while they are in prison.

The Huffington Post reports:

Across the U.S. and beyond, inmates are using social networks and the growing numbers of smartphones smuggled into prisons and jails to harass their victims or accusers and intimidate witnesses. California corrections officials who monitor social networking sites said they have found many instances in which inmates taunted victims or made unwanted sexual advances.

If you do choose to participate in social media, make sure that you use it in a manner that keeps you safe. Understand your privacy settings and keep up with the constant changes in privacy policies.

Still A Perilous World Out There

For those of us who grew up with the threat of the atom bomb, today's threats of cyberwarfare, terrorist attacks, and extreme weather are just *plus ça change, plus c'est la même chose.* Now, as then, we must be prepared. Becoming a connoisseur in all those area that affect our safety is essential for living safely today.

Connoisseur Rich

FORTY YEARS BEFORE the film *How To Steal A Million* gave us a cinematic connoisseur, mystery fiction provided even more true-to-life portraits. The American writer Willard Huntington Wright who published in the 1920s and 1930s under the pseudonym S. S. Van Dine was himself an art connoisseur. His fictional sleuth, the art connoisseur par excellence Philo Vance, was his *alter ego*.

The art connoisseur author and his fictional creation are important here because in both we see how knowledge and experience of quality can help us become rich.

Willard Huntington Wright attended Harvard and later studied art in Munich and Paris. He was literary and art critic, journalist and magazine editor without great financial success. In 1923 he suffered what Chris Steinbrunner and Otto Penzler in their *Encyclopedia of Mystery and Detection* describe as a "severe breakdown." The cure the doctors prescribed was bed rest. This confinement continued for two years during which WHW was forbidden any scholarly study. He read mystery fiction and amassed a collection of 2000 volumes.

As someone who for more than 40 years of her adult life has used reading mystery fiction of the pre-World War II Golden Age (and a cup of hot tea) as the antidote for stress and exhaustion, I can testify to the restorative benefits of the reading material chosen.

WHW decided he would write mystery fiction of a superior quality appealing to a more intelligent and well-educated readership than the works of many mystery writers he had surveyed. He used his knowledge and experience of art and combined it with his analysis of mystery fiction to create his own subgenre. He also saw mystery fiction as a vehicle through which he could promote the modern art and literature about which he felt so passionate.

As S. S. Van Dine, the writer presented an extensive synopsis of the first three Philo Vance mystery novels to Scribner's "editor of genius" Maxwell Perkins. The books were accepted. The first Philo Vance mystery *The Benson Murder Case* was published in 1926, the same year Maxwell Perkins edited Ernest Hemingway's novel *The Sun Also Rises*. Coincidentally, 1926 was also the year that Agatha Christie published her most popular Hercule Poirot mystery novel *The Murder of Roger Ackroyd*.

Five more Philo Vance mysteries followed the *Benson Case* from that 1926 beginning until 1939, the year of the author's death. In those years, the worldwide popularity of the Philo Vance mysteries made his creator very wealthy. The J. K. Rowling of his day.

The fictional sleuth Philo Vance helped define connoisseur in the public consciousness. Readers first see the detective in his New York penthouse apartment decorated with his priceless and extensive art collection that ranges from Michelangelo to Picasso and includes Asian and African art. The penthouse is the top two floors of a beautifully remodeled old mansion. Philo Vance is waited on by his proper English servant who serves as butler, valet, major-domo and specialty cook. As the story begins, Currie is preparing his employer a late breakfast of strawberries and Eggs Benedict and his incomparable coffee.

One avenue to wealth followed by connoisseurs is seeing value in items others have not yet recognized. The connoisseur makes an early purchase that appreciates in value. In the reader's first glimpse of Philo Vance, he is perusing a catalog from the Paris art dealer Vollard making selections of Cézanne watercolors he wishes to purchase. Philo Vance was a fictional character serving as his author's voice. Ambroise Vollard was a real person, one the foremost art dealers of the early 20th century and champion of avant-garde artists. Some of you likely saw *Cézanne to Picasso: Ambroise Vollard, Patron of the Avant-Garde,* a special exhibit staged by The Metropolitan Museum of Art. Philo Vance tells his lawyer arranging the purchase of the Cézannes: "They're very beautiful and valuable little knickknacks, and rather inexpensive when one considers what they'll be bringing in a few years. Really an excellent investment for some money-loving soul."

The reader is told that Philo Vance purchased two Cézanne watercolors, one for $250 and another for $300, and in four years their value tripled to $750 and $900. In the spring of 2007 Sotheby's auctioned one of Vollard's Cézanne watercolors "Still Life With Green Melon." The painting brought $25.5 million.

During the Dust Bowl of the 1930s, a woman who was later my neighbor, received a small inheritance. Her husband suffered health problems and the family income was small. She could have used her inheritance for necessities and a few luxuries. Instead she drove her Model A to West Texas where the drought-ravaged land was selling for 50 cents an acre. In the part of Oklahoma she lived they were discovering oil. She believed there was surely oil under that Texas land too. If not, there would be other uses to which she could put it. In fact, she was right about the oil. Even after her death, her grandchildren were still cashing oil royalty checks.

For some *Chic & Slim* Connoisseurs, it will be the big coup: art or real estate or stock that increases tenfold or more in a few years. For others, the benefits will be incremental and cumulative over the long term. The decades of consistently finding some quality item at a moving sale, resale shop, stuffed in a dumpster, something a friend is discarding and using it in place of one that otherwise would have to be bought at retail. Buying a well-constructed home so that instead of constantly paying for repairs and high utility bills, you can put money into low risk investments that will pay off over time and bring a secure worry-free retirement. The unsexy long term investment often pays best.

The author of the Philo Vance mysteries provides two more useful lessons about connoisseurship and wealth. Income from the Philo Vance books, films, serials, and translations brought wealth. But Willard Huntington Wright squandered the money on a lavish lifestyle. His drug addiction is believed have been responsible for the decline in the quality and popularity of his work. In a decade and a half his wealth was gone and he was dead at age 50.

Whether a connoisseur earns income in the thousands or the millions, to become rich, spending must not exceed income. (Many Americans have not yet learned this basic rule.) Buy the best quality that you can afford. I repeat: *afford*. If what you buy might be repossessed or foreclosed on—or if the interest is going to double the cost, rethink your purchase.

Another Basic Rule: Plan ahead for major necessity purchases. Saving for a later purchase may seem old-fashioned. Yet, even if you can afford a new refrigerator or vehicle on your income, you will get better value for your money if you have time for comparison shopping. Before you make any purchase ask two questions: Do I *really* need it? Will I *really* use it?

Closets and garages of America overflow with purchases that never got much use. Electric woks. Countertop grills. Foot massagers. Will your purchase meet a real need, or is it just the *gadget du jour* that will take up space in the garage after the third use? Think of all the products you bought that you did not use. How much money would you have saved if you had *not* bought them and put the money into savings or a good investment?

Some "dream" purchases, turn out to be much trouble and little pleasure. A man who learned by experience mused about an expensive power boat he bought: "You think the day you buy that boat is the happiest day of your life. But it isn't. The happiest day of your life is the day you sell the damn thing."

Another in mid-life bought the sports car he dreamed of when a teenager. He really did not enjoy driving it. He preferred another vehicle for errands and vacation. For the most part, his sports car sat in the garage under a tarp. His cats found it cozy for naps. His dream car turned out to be a $70,000 cat bed.

If you regularly spend money on products you never use or which do nothing to improve your quality of life, you might read *Affluenza: The All-*

Consuming Epidemic by John De Graaf, David Wann and Thomas H. Naylor. In the section on treatment in Chapter 22, the authors strongly recommend "bed rest." Consider that it was bed rest that put the connoisseur who created Philo Vance on the road to wealth.

Addiction & Wealth

Poor health or addiction can sabotage wealth. You have a better chance of becoming rich or keeping wealth you have if you are healthy, mentally alert, and vigorous. And free from addictions. Sensible moderate eating, exercise, adequate rest and avoiding unhealthy behavior promote good health. Countless lives and finances have been ruined by addiction. Countless individuals have radically improved their lives and finances when they cured their addiction.

You might not think that a junk food addiction could have much effect on your finances. Yet one *Chic & Slim* woman emailed that when she stopped overeating junk food, not only did she become slimmer (size 16 down to size 4), but the money she did not spend on junk food paid for regular facials, manicures and pedicures that previously she could not afford.

Some seeming addictions, such as mine to hot tea, can actually be beneficial. For me tea drinking is a restorative behavior. My afternoon pot of tea and a small pastry or sandwich has been sufficient to satisfy for decades. Research has shown health benefits including preventing heart disease, fighting certain cancers and boosting the immune system. It certainly helps me deal with stress. I would not be half as productive a writer without my afternoon tea.

Addictions, such as those to shopping, online games, genre fiction, television viewing, telephone chatting can have a detrimental effect on finances. How do you determine whether an activity is a restorative leisure time activity or an addiction? Professor Mark Griffiths, who studies behavioral addictions at Nottingham Trent University in England, told *USA Today* that to count as a real addiction a behavior has to be destructive, cause withdrawal symptoms and prompt ever greater use to maintain the kick.

"Lots of people display some of those components, but very few display all of them, and in that sense, to me, they are not classically addicted," Griffiths said.

I doubt many reading *Chic & Slim* books spend 12 hours a day online playing *World of Warcraft*. But there may be activities, while not technically addictions, on which you spend time that might be better spent to improve your bank balance. I have known women that are so addicted to reading romance novels that they will spend great amounts of money on convenience foods because preparing meals would mean they had to put down their book and cook.

Before US Postal Service Carrier Pickup, I spent much time standing in line at the post office to ship the *Chic & Slim* books. A woman frequently also in line to ship packages I learned was an online shopping addict. She ordered incessantly. But she sent back *all* the merchandise she ordered. What more productive things she might have done than stand in line at the post office several days a week? (Though she may now be using Carrier Pickup too.) What might she buy with that money she spends on return postage? One would hope items or services that would give her real use and pleasure? Keep a time diary for two or three days. You may want to give some activities less of your valuable time.

Quality To Save And Earn

We know the benefits of quality. Quality products save you money because they last longer. You spend less time doing product research and shopping. You spend less for maintenance and repairs. Quality tools do a better job than poor ones, enabling the user to save or make money. Quality items are more pleasurable to wear and use. They have more aesthetically pleasing design.

If there are so many obvious advantages to quality, why do Americans spend so much money buying junk?

First of all, many Americans today with enough disposable income to afford quality did not grow up with quality items. They do not have the quality habit. Nor the quality taste. When I lived in Corpus Christi, between

HEB and Sun Harvest there was a wonderful choice of quality food. Some friends who had the income that they could have bought all the fresh fruits and vegetables and quality meats they wanted still bought white supermarket bread, canned soups, canned refried beans, sliced processed (faux) cheese on which they had subsisted in less affluent days. They took a cruise on a French luxury liner and after two nights of the two-star chef's seven-course dinners, asked if instead they could have a hamburger. Knowing how a French chef would feel about having his menu rejected in favor of *le hamburger*, I am surprised my friends were not pitched overboard.

The tendency for instant gratification that causes Americans to overeat junk food, also drives them to buy poor quality consumer products. They tell themselves they will use the lesser quality until they can afford or make a decision on real quality. One difference I notice between Americans and Europeans is that Europeans generally do not subscribe to the something cheap until we can buy better idea. If they cannot afford a quality item, they simply do without until they can afford it. They buy a quality item with the idea that it will last decades, possibly their entire lifetime, and can be passed on to their children and grandchildren.

Decades ago, before columnist Michelle Singletary, there was another woman who wrote a financial advice column for the *Washington Post*. I have forgotten her name, but I remember her advice: When you think you absolutely have to have something, you can probably do without it.

Because of her advice, many times in my life when I thought I absolutely had to have some item for work or my personal life, I would delay the purchase. If I could maintain reasonable efficiency without the item, then I crossed it off my shopping list.

If more people followed that columnist's advice, our landfills might not be overflowing. But doing without is not something Americans do much any more. Not with installment buying, credit cards and home equity loans.

Is Quality Really Expensive?

The perception is that quality is expensive. Some quality items are very, very expensive. In the long-term, however, many quality items cost less than their mediocre versions. For instance, buying a vacuum with a retractable cord instead of a less expensive model whose cord must be rewound by hand after each use. Think how much time it will save you over the years and what you will do with that time saved. This becomes especially meaningful if you need more time for relaxing because of your mental or physical health, or if you are self-employed and, for you, time equals money. Remember that if you can cut only five minutes from your regular activities every day of the year, at the end of the year you have gained more than 30 hours for yourself. Just think what you could do in 30 hours. Cut 10 minutes, get 60 hours.

Ranking Not A Good Indicator of Quality

Quality often has no connection to ranking. American companies love to tout their products as "bestselling" or "most popular." In the USA where true quality is not particularly valued, selling the most of any item may have little to do with excellence.

Quality is enduring. "Most sold" is temporary and frequently changing. In the USA, ranking more often reflects money spent on advertising, not quality. There are exceptions to this general rule. My much-loved iPod is one. Apple spends liberally advertising the iPod. Nonetheless, the MP3 player is excellent quality and an aid in my efforts to help people live chic, slim, safe and rich lives.

Quality Gives Control

A chief benefit for the *Chic & Slim* Connoisseur is quality products give us better control over our lives. Quality appliances save us time and energy without extracting a high price of frustration.

A quality vehicle delivers us to our destination in safety and comfort, at least if we drive the vehicle in a reasonably sensible manner. Quality food satisfies nutritionally, emotionally, and aesthetically and (assuming we chose a balanced diet and moderate portions) maintains health and gives an attractive appearance. Quality clothing and accessories make you feel rich even when you are not. Quality can free you of feelings of emptiness. True quality products and experiences, sometimes moderately priced or free, can make you satisfied and confident.

No matter the satisfaction and service quality products give you, if you are miserable, your work will suffer. You will spend on compensations for your misery. For that reason, to become rich, you must become a connoisseur in three more areas.

Connoisseur of People Experiences Places PEP

Have you ever found yourself in a place you hated, among people you could not stand, with an enforced schedule of detested activities? You dreaded to get up in the morning. Getting through the day was an effort. Dealing with offensive people and activities in an offensive place sapped your energy and made you want to crawl in some dark space and lie there.

That describes your life right now, you say? Oh dear!

How different when you are in a location you find delightful and perfectly in sync with your favored lifestyle. What joy it is when you are among people you like, doing activities that you enjoy. You feel energized and never tired. You are full of pep, to use a short little word for that happy invigorating energy you feel.

Connoisseur of People

We all know individuals who consistently choose quality in the food they eat, the clothes they wear, their home, its decor, their vacation locations, the schools they and their children attend, the music they listen to, the books they read, the films they see. But they surround themselves with people that make them miserable and drain the life out them—like vampires, as the author Albert Bernstein describes them in his book *Emotional Vampires: Dealing With People Who Drain You Dry*. Lillian Glass labeled them toxic people in her book *Toxic People: 10 Ways Of Dealing With People Who Make Your Life Miserable*.

We need quality people in our life, just as we need quality food, apparel, and appliances and services.

True, a poorly designed, troublesome kitchen appliance can frustrate our breakfast time. An incompetent yardman can butcher your boxwood hedge. But you can replace the toaster. The boxwood will grow back. These are nothing in comparison to the misery that malicious people can cause.

Because what those people damage is our very selves.

Any person who would fall into the category either of "vampire" or "toxic" would not make the cut of quality people we want in our life. But it may be difficult to avoid many people. Among these are coworkers and family members. The two books mentioned above (as well as others) can give you help in dealing with these people.

Experience has taught me that, as much as possible, it is best to avoid people who make us unhappy or angry or feel bad about ourselves or, perhaps worst of all, who drive us to seek refuge in overindulgence in substances and activities not good for us. Too many people soothe the hurt from the hostility of others with comfort food. Cheesecake as a balm for put-downs.

In the original *Chic & Slim: How Those Chic French Women Eat All That Rich Food And Still Stay Slim*, I counseled you that if you wanted to be slim, it was best to associate with slim people rather than fat people. You will be influenced by good food habits of the slim and avoid the pressure of bad food habits of the fat.

Now as I write this *Connoisseur* book, we have the report of a major study by Dr. Nicholas Christakis, a physician and professor of medical sociology at Harvard Medical School, and James Fowler, an associate professor of political science at the University of California in San Diego. Their study found precisely what I had advised you a decade ago.

Dr. Fowler was quoted in the *International Herald Tribune* saying: "So why not make friends with a thin person, and let the thin person's behavior influence you and your obese friend?" Choose people you associate with carefully. They can affect your happiness, and your hip measurement. Chic, slim French women I knew had limited social circles. They did not join organizations or women's groups as American women so often do.

Quality is perhaps not the best word to define people who would be the most beneficial in our lives. Quality carries an older meaning: people who have attained the highest social position. Any number of people who might be very good for us have absolutely no social position whatsoever. I prefer art historian and critic Bernard Berenson's term "life-enhancing" people.

In the book *One Special Summer*, the account of Jacqueline and Lee Bouvier's vacation in Europe the summer of 1951, the sisters, who would a decade later be known to the world as Jacqueline Kennedy and Lee Radziwill, recount a visit they made to Bernard Berenson at his villa *I Tatti* outside Florence. The art critic advised the young women not to waste their time on what he called "life-diminishing" people. They should concentrate on associating with those who were "life-enhancing."

In the early 19th century, the German philosopher Goethe had used the term "life-enhancing" for art. A century later, early in his career, Bernard Berenson used the same term defining "life-enhancing" art as that which "makes one feel more hopefully, more zestfully alive; living more intense, more radiant a life not only physically but morally and spiritually as well; reaching out to the topmost peak of our capacities, contented with no satisfaction lower than the highest..."

In his eighties, that summer when the Bouvier sisters visited him at his home in Italy, Bernard Berenson had extended this concept of life-enhancing to people. By his definition, a life-enhancing person would be one who made us feel more hopeful with more enthusiasm for life itself. Life-enhancing people would make us want to live more moral and spiritual lives, and to strive to achieve the best of our abilities. Life-enhancing people would encourage us to make quality the standard for all our possessions and experiences.

Bernard Berenson was one of the best-known connoisseurs of the 20th century. His biography by Ernest Samuels published by Harvard University Press is titled *Bernard Berenson: The Making of a Connoisseur*. That same advice this connoisseur offered to the young sisters Jacqueline and Lee Bouvier is an excellent standard for us to apply as we become connoisseurs of people.

Connoisseur of Experiences
If you want to be chic, slim, safe and rich, another area in which you must become a connoisseur is experience.

One good sign I see in the USA is that many people are becoming less focused on having a lot of stuff. Instead they are choosing a moderate number of possessions that allow them to enjoy quality experiences. Downsizing in homes is one trend. Selling that huge house with the park-size yard whose maintenance seemed to devour every weekend, and moving to a maintenance-free condo, or a small "greener" house frees them for more travel, more time to read, more time for hobbies and exercise, more time with family and friends— more time to relax and enjoy life.

When I first began to meet and socialize with Europeans about 40 years ago, I became aware how more focused my friends in the USA were on material things. They frantically pursued larger, more luxurious cars and the bigger, more expensive houses in more upscale neighborhoods. They bought the latest appliances and personal gadgets. They smothered their children with trendy toys. They filled their closets with clothes, many they never seemed to wear. My American friends seemed to have little time for anything besides work and shopping for more stuff.

The Europeans, however, were into quality experiences. That was just as well since most of them seemed to live in places that lacked space for many possessions. If my European friends bought all that stuff my American friends were buying, they would not have had any place to put it or park it.

Europeans preferred a delicious meal with friends, idling over drinks in a café, going to the beach with the children, discussing the latest books and films, and traveling. When I observed how content they seemed, as well as how slim and attractively dressed, that convinced me that enjoying quality experiences was better than having lots of possessions. This philosophy put me somewhat out of sync with my fellow Americans when I returned to live in the USA. But as the years have passed, I have seen so many Americans changing from possession-centered lives to ones that value spending time in ways that bring pleasure and relief from stress. That is not to say that most Americans are anywhere near the ideal European quality of life. But I have seen healthy progress in recent years.

So how do we become *Chic & Slim* Connoisseurs of experience?

Here too, it seems that Bernard Berenson's life-enhancing/life-diminishing is a useful standard. Before we embark on an activity, we need to ask the question: Will this experience enhance my life? You should apply this standard to the mundane as well as the major. Take a simple daily act such as teeth brushing. Definitely this activity makes life better. If you do not brush your teeth, all sorts of life-diminishing results may occur. Bad breath (there goes your chance for a date with that attractive man you just met), time and expense of dental office visits, discomfort of fillings or extractions. Root canals. Crowns. Bridges. Implants. Becoming a toothless crone? Oh, dear!

What about a choice between staying home and watching a DVD or attending a chamber music performance by Juilliard graduates? If you detest classical music, you are going to derive more life-enhancing pleasure and relaxation from the DVD.

But if your boss invites you to hear his daughter, a Juilliard graduate, perform Schubert, and you hope for a bonus that will finance a trip to the Sundance Film Festival, your life, in the long run, may be better enhanced by choosing the chamber music.

Don't be shortsighted looking for the enhancement. Or the diminishment. Attending the daughter's concert will not guarantee the bonus. There are no absolutely "right" answers.

Among the observations I made when I began my study of French women and their techniques for staying slim and dressing chic was they way they performed tasks. So different from the American women I had observed growing up. The American women tended to do everything in a rushed manner with no thought for the quality of the act performed. Whether it was dressing for a party or doing the supper dishes, the attitude just seemed to be: get it over with. American women often did not strive for excellence.

Yet French women, I observed, strove for excellence in *everything* they did, even the simplest and most everyday tasks. Every act was performed with concentration and care. Applying lipstick. Setting the table. Tying a scarf. Arranging themselves in a chair at a sidewalk cafe. Gazing at the man across the table.

I also became aware that so many American women I observed took little pleasure in their activities. French women, on the other hand, seemed to take pleasure from every activity. They arranged their lives so as not to do things that did not give them pleasure. Cecilia Sarkozy, the former wife of French president Nicholas Sarkozy, gave a dramatic demonstration of the lengths to which French women will go to avoid activities that do not give them pleasure. Mme Sarkozy had made no secret that she took no pleasure in the duties of First Lady of France. Her divorce freed her from any expectation that she perform those duties.

Doing What You Want

Another necessity for quality life experiences is successfully dealing with the problem of doing what you want to do versus what someone else wants you to do. All my life I have heard people complain about having to do things that they hate because their spouse or friend or child insisted. It does not seem to occur to these people that there might be another choice.

One of my friends who likes arty European cinema is married to a man whose taste in films is car chases and things blowing up. Early in their marriage she persuaded him to attend a showing of an art film. Ten minutes of enigmatic perspective shots and obtuse subtitles and he leaned toward her and said, "I'll meet you at the popcorn counter in an hour and a half." And he left.

They have many common interests that have sustained four decades of marriage. But following that first art film, they agreed that attending such films is something that she would do without him. Of course Netflix has solved the problem nicely. My friend can watch her films on DVD while her husband is doing something useful, like varnishing the sailboat or cleaning out the garage.

Often today I see this scenario featuring two family members: The first has followed a healthy lifestyle. Nutritious, moderate eating for normal weight, exercise and rest, no smoking, limited or no alcohol consumption.

A good education and hard work has paid off in savings and investments. The second family member has lived on junk food and cigarettes and abused alcohol. Exercise has consisted of shopping at the mall and changing channels with the remote control. Not wanting to put out the effort for higher education, jobs have been low-paying. Expenditures have always exceeded income. Now they are overweight and suffering serious health and financial problems.

The first family member who has lived responsibly is ready to enjoy a well-earned retirement. But they are constantly being called on by the other family member to drive them to medical appointments and stay with them at the hospital for their surgeries and do household chores when they are recuperating. Because the irresponsible family member's money is limited, the more affluent family member ends up paying for everything from the fuel for transportation to bills that less responsible family member cannot.

This is *not* a new problem.

The fable of the ant and the grasshopper is an old, old story. We know how it ends. The ant lived comfortably through the winter and felt no compunction to help out the grasshopper. The grasshopper starved and died. But you may not feel comfortable being that tough on your sister— even if she has ignored your warnings and advice all these years.

You, like countless others, may be faced with the question of how much you should allow the quality of life for which you have worked hard to be diminished by bad choices made by someone else who calls on you for help.

You may want to set boundaries and define how much time and money you are willing to devote to another's aid.

Unless you set some limits, that money you so carefully saved may go to pay the bills for someone who squandered their own money. Instead of enjoying life-enhancing experiences, you may put in a lot of hours as an unpaid home health care worker.

Never All Rose Gardens

Not every life-enhancing experience will be a pleasure, however. In hindsight, I recognize that some rewarding experiences were, at the time, exhausting and miserable. I remember a West African train trip decades ago from central Ivory Coast to Ouagadougou, (then) Upper Volta. The bench in the bumping train was unbelievably hard, the train restroom unbelievably filthy, the odor of the antiquated, un–air–conditioned train was gagging. The night was long, sleepless and miserably uncomfortable. But at dawn, as I watched the sun spread soft tentative light over the vast empty expanse of African savannah, I felt I knew what it must have been like at dawn on the first day of Creation. A powerful, moving experience that was worth every second of miserable discomfort that preceded it.

Time passes quickly and most of us have so many things we wish to do in our lifetimes. I assure you that when you reach your 60s as I am now, you will review your life and wish that you had not allowed yourself or others to waste even one precious minute.

To live richly, you must be a connoisseur of experience. You must choose experiences thoughtfully. You must not allow yourself to be only a "badminton shuttlecock" batted from one activity to another by the wishes and demands of others.

Connoisseur of Places

I have long been a connoisseur of places. By the time I was five, I had traveled overland from the center of the USA where I was born to its northwestern corner and back, and from that center to the Los Angles area and back, also overland, by the desert route.

By the time I was sixteen, I had traveled to New York City by a route that took me through 15 states. I had visited Canada and Mexico. This travel convinced me there were many interesting places in the world. I wanted to visit as many as possible. I wanted to live in exotic places. As soon as I finished college I began my worldwide odyssey. I have lived in those exotic places. Vacationing is wonderful. Living in a new locale gives experiences not possible from a visit. A vacation, I once read, is like having a few dates, living somewhere is like a long-term relationship.

Every year *Money* magazine publishes its best places to live in the USA list. There are sublists too: Most Singles, Affordable Homes, Skinniest. Just as it is easier to be chic if those around you are chic, you will find it easier to be slim if the lifestyle is conducive to normal weight and you are living among people of healthy weight. That generally means the availability of fresh fruits and vegetables and easy access to regular exercise and weather that allows for some form of enjoyable outdoor exercise all year long.

Many locations offer healthy outdoor activities. Many people living in these locations choose to watch television indoors.

Living in a safe location used to mean living where the crime rate was low. Now it also means living somewhere that would be unattractive to terrorists. We look today for a place low on likely terrorist target lists and low-crime, yet one that offers the amenities that we want.

If you want to make money, you must to go where money is. Previously true. But with the Internet, it is now possible to live anywhere you have a good Internet connection and make sufficient money to live well and accumulate savings. The requirement is that you have a product or service that you can deliver from whatever location you place yourself. High tech communications has made it possible to live almost anywhere.

But if the place isn't the right place for you, it doesn't matter how well dressed or slim the locals, or how safe, nor how good for earning a living. If you are miserable, you may neglect your appearance and overeat to compensate for your misery. Safe isn't always worth being bored numb. If you are somewhere you absolutely hate, you probably won't do the best job at your work. You likely will not become rich.

Several months ago I received an email.

Dear Anne, For as long as I can remember I had this dream to live in New York City. About two years ago I finally made the move to the big city from California. I had ordered your books sometime in 2002, and from that point began to live the chic and slim lifestyle. My favorite part of the day was my tea hour. I really learned how to enjoy the pleasures of life and to cultivate a personal style.

However, when I finally moved to New York, my dream of the big city became more of a nightmare. I discovered that New York was not exactly glamorous (especially on a tight budget). The stress and constant intensity of city life completely engulfed me, and to make a long story short, I lost the pleasure in real living.

As a result of trying to keep up with the rat race, I let myself go. No time for tea. No time for style. No time for me! I convinced my husband to move up to the suburbs in the hope of finding some sort of balance, but I was literally so burned out from the city that I continued to unravel. I miss the beach, the sunshine, and having a little garden. We've decided to move back to California this summer, and the thought of it has given me the extra boost that I needed to snap myself back together. I have been re-reading your books, and making conscious decisions to slow down and enjoy life once more. I am so grateful for those books. Thank you so very much for your chic and slim guidance! Sincerely, Meredith

Sometimes the place we dream about doesn't turn out to be as we dreamed it. Sometimes by the time we arrive at our dream place, it has changed. The pace of life in some cities can be exhausting, as Meredith commented in her email. The pace of life around you can take away your pleasure. Today, there are any number of vibrant cities that unless you are truly affluent, the struggle to make enough money to pay for the necessities leaves you too exhausted to enjoy life. Better to live somewhere you can afford and have some leisure. Make visits to the place of your dreams.

I have friends who love theater. They cannot afford to live in the style they prefer in New York City or London, but the moderate cost of living where they reside and work allows them to spend a week in New York or London seeing the new plays almost every year.

In contemplating a relocation, an important question is: Can I afford to live there? Answer that question first. Relocate with a sense of adventure. Relocate with the idea that no place is likely to remain wonderful forever. When I moved to Corpus Christi, it was the absolute perfect place for me to live and to write the *Chic & Slim* books. Then, the situation changed. Time to move. I moved. I will likely move again.

So many wonderful places. So little time.

Today people move. People move a lot. Hardly any American lives a lifetime in the town or city in which they were born. Certainly not the same neighborhood.

Become a *Chic & Slim* Connoisseur of places. Choose locations that will give you the best quality of life and a generous income to enjoy your life. When you are in a place you love, with people you enjoy, doing what you love to do, then you are truly rich.

Traditional or Chic & Slim Connoisseur

In 1923, Willard Huntington Wright began his bed rest with voracious mystery novel reading that would inspire the creation of his art connoisseur sleuth Philo Vance and make the author wealthy.

That same year, on the other side of the Atlantic, a British author Dorothy L. Sayers published the first of her series of mystery novels about another connoisseur sleuth, Lord Peter Wimsey.

Just as the S. S. Van Dine–Philo Vance mystery novels were written to a high literary standard, so were those of this Oxford-educated scholarly author. Like the Philo Vance books, the Lord Peter Wimsey mysteries earned their author a generous income.

No doubt Dorothy L. Sayers' connoisseur detective who first appeared in 1923 provided inspiration for Philo Vance who made his debut in 1926. Lord Peter Wimsey is wealthy, aristocratic, intellectual, suave, attired in the finest Savile Row tailoring, and living elegantly with a manservant in an apartment described as a "block of new, perfect and expensive flats." Lord Peter is a connoisseur of rare books and the author describes the room in which he displays his collection:

Lord Peter's library was one of the most delightful bachelor rooms in London. Its scheme was black and primrose; its walls were lined with rare editions, and its chairs and Chesterfield sofa suggested the embraces of the houris. In one corner stood a black baby grand, a wood fire leaped on a wide old-fashioned hearth, and the Sèvres vases on the chimneypiece were filled with ruddy and gold chrysanthemums. . . . it seemed . . . like a colourful and gilded paradise in a mediæval painting.

When the reader first sees the detective, he is on his way to a sale to purchase additions to his collection. The reader is told that Lord Peter already owns excellent printed Dantes, though the finest has no provenance and that he may have acquired it by "stealth." The author also tells the reader that Lord Peter is mistaken in thinking that there is another copy in the Vatican of 'Four Sons of Aymon' he wants to bid on at the sale. Actually, Dorothy L. Sayers, a Dante scholar, assures us that the one other existing copy is not in the Vatican as Lord Peter believes, but in the collection of Earl Spencer.

Lord Peter Wimsey was a fictional detective, but the Earl Spencer mentioned was a real person: the 7th Earl Spencer, grandfather of the woman we know as Diana, Princess of Wales.

While I find the Philo Vance character in the S. S. Van Dine novels so obnoxious that I have never been able to finish one of the mysteries, I enjoy Dorothy L. Sayers' Lord Peter Wimsey. I have read and reread the novels and seen many times the excellent BBC productions starring Ian Carmichael as Lord Peter.

Dorothy L. Sayers was much more sensible and prudent about the money she earned from Lord Peter than Willard Huntington Wright was about the money he earned from Philo Vance. Whatever addictions Dorothy L. Sayers had, (she was a smoker and had a tendency to overeat) she continued to live well and work productively. She achieved the best kind of wealth, that which gives financial security for the life and work we want most. Often quoted is Miss Sayers' advice to women about life, money and surviving difficulties:

> The best remedy for a bruised heart is not, as so many people seem
> to think, repose upon a manly bosom. Much more efficacious are
> honest work, physical activity, and the sudden acquisition of Wealth.

These words appear at the beginning of *Have His Carcase*, the 1932 Lord Peter Wimsey mystery. Harriet Vane, the fictional detective novel writer who is very much Dorothy L. Sayers' *alter ego,* solos in the first 46 pages of the book before Lord Peter appears. She has recently found herself with a comfortable amount of wealth.

No fortuitous inheritance, rather her hard work has paid off and her books are selling well—boosted by publicity of her exoneration from a murder charge. She has signed lucrative contracts on two continents for future books.

Biographer James Brabazon says that Dorothy L. Sayers, through Harriet Vane, was able to express her own thoughts, perceptions and emotions, her own vision of the world. In this mystery, the author shares with women her wisdom about love and money.

Harriet's books are earning her a substantial income. Yet she does not give herself a pampering stay at a resort or set herself up in luxurious living and party with her friends. Instead she sets out on a solitary June walking holiday along the English coast, sensibly dressed, traveling light, and free from "forwarded letters." (Today that would translate as leaving her iPhone at home.) For someone who earns her living by creative, sedentary work, this is the perfect restorative vacation. The bracing sea air, physical exercise and solitude will benefit her physical and mental health. She can refill the creative well for new fiction. Dorothy L. Sayers knew that earning income for a comfortable life required taking care of your health, spending moderately and continuing to gain the knowledge and experience that translated into quality work.

Cinderella? Or Nicole & Harriet?

Some of us grew up being sold the Cinderella fable: A fairy godmother appears and provides an impoverished young woman with stunning clothes and luxury transportation, sends her to an exclusive event where she meets a handsome prince who falls madly in love with her on first sight, pursues her, and ultimately whisks her off to live a life of luxury and ease.

Neither Nicole Bonnet in *How To Steal A Million,* nor Harriet Vane in the Lord Peter Wimsey mysteries are Cinderellas. They set out to solve their problems and insure the quality of their lives through their own efforts.

True, they have some assistance. But Nicole does not expect Simon to take care of the problem for her. She participates. She helps with reconnaissance and planning. She even takes off the Givenchy, dons cleaning lady clothes, gets down on her knees and scrubs the museum floor. Harriet Vane is even more active in insuring her own happiness and financial well-being.

Chic & Slim Connoisseurship & You

The *best* things in life may be free. But the necessities such as food, shelter, clothing, medicines and those pampering treatments that benefit your appearance and mental well-being cost money. Like the fictional Nicole Bonnet and Harriet Vane, and the real life Dorothy L. Sayers, you, as a connoisseur, can achieve the slim body, chic personal style, safety and financial security you seek through your own clever efforts. Forget Cinderella. It's more fun to be Nicole or Harriet and be part of the action.

Of course no one becomes a connoisseur overnight, or from reading one article. The knowledge and experience to become a connoisseur in any area takes time and effort. Yet, with information technologies today, connoisseurship can come with an ease and speed unimaginable even a decade ago. Your efforts toward becoming a *Chic & Slim* Connoisseur, rather than being drudgery, can give meaning and richness to your life. As a *Chic & Slim* Connoisseur using quality, you may become rich in more ways than you imagined.

Connoisseur Rich Today

THE ORIGINAL *CONNOISSEUR* was published in the spring of 2008. By autumn of that year the Great Recession, as that time of economic crisis came to be known, was in full swing. Some think our economic hard times are not yet over. Unemployment remains high and the middle class finds itself increasingly pinched. A college education, that passport to a financially stable life, grows more prohibitively expensive. Graduates forced to finance higher education with student loans face years of burdensome debt. In many regions of the world the economic situation is still in crisis mode.

How did my theories about connoisseurship in aid of riches hold up for me during these five years of economically difficult times? The answer in two words: very well.

As I pointed out early in the Rich section of the original version of this book, a connoisseur using specialized knowledge of quality frequently is able to purchase something valuable at a low price by recognizing value that others do not see. Sometimes, as with property, the connoisseur increases the intrinsic value by making improvements. When the market for that particular item rises, the connoisseur gains substantial return on the investment. In the meantime the connoisseur has the pleasure and use of the acquisition. Other times, all that is necessary is holding the item for a time until the market places higher value. Remember my examples of the paintings and of the neighbor who bought the West Texas land for 50 cents an acre during the Depression.

In 2009 I finally located a property that met most of what I required in a home. True, I would surely have found a more satisfactory property if I had been able to wait several months longer. But for reasons of health and safety, relocation as soon as possible was necessary. The first 18 months at this new property presented the same problems with noise as in the neighborhood I left—though, happily, the new noisy neighbors did not have pyromaniac tendencies. Since my second year here at the new place, noise problems have been largely solved.

Despite that, with a little more time, I might have found a better property at a better price, my connoisseur's knowledge of early 20th century houses has gained me a house that has required little expenditure for structural repairs. I have been able to reduce the amount I spend on shelter and utilities. A small investment in weatherproofing cut gas and electric bills. The severe drought here in Texas the past several years has limited my ability to raise as many vegetables as I had planned. So I haven't achieved the savings on the food bill I had hoped. But my herbs have flourished. All winter long I have been harvesting my *roquette* (arugula) for tasty salads. The garden gives me great pleasure as I carry out my landscape redesign. My current location is the most conducive to my work of any place I have lived. As a consequence, my income has risen. (Income had suffered in the previous two locations because night noise lead to sleep deprivation and hindered productivity.) Since coming to this location, I have written a new book, created digital versions of several *Chic & Slim* books and am in the progress of updating and digitizing this book. I am taking pleasure in restoring and decorating my house.

Because of my policy of buying quality clothing combined with a personal style based on classic rather than trendy, my monetary outlay for clothing these past five years has been small. Especially because staying slim has made me the recipient of quality clothing others give away because they gained too much weight to wear them.

One recent item I have been given is a pair of hardly-worn black leather pants, that must-have item in the wardrobes of chic French women. I already had a black leather skirt, another item passed on to me by a woman who could not squeeze into this beautiful and expensive skirt.

My connoisseur emphasis on quality has allowed me to live better, save more and work more productively during this period that has been difficult for many other Americans who suffered job losses, foreclosures, bankruptcies, ravages of credit card debt and loss of retirement funds.

Defense Against Scammers and Exploiters

If we want to be rich, a first line of defense must be against those who would scam and exploit us. But unless there are regulations that prevent (and punish when necessary) banks and investment and credit card companies from deceiving us with print so small it requires the Hubble telescope to read it, phrased in language so confusing that you would need the 19th century French team that finally deciphered Egyptian hieroglyphics to figure out what was meant, even we as connoisseur consumers don't have much chance of protecting ourselves.

When in 2009 the chickens came home to roost from risky mortgages and devious credit card policies, it became evident that these not only put individuals in dire straits, these risky and devious policies could throw economies worldwide into turmoil. Something needed to be done.

One thing done was the establishment of the Bureau of Consumer Financial Protection as part of financial reform legislation passed by the US Congress. The bureau has been successful in punishing and in preventing abuses such as those that lead to the recent Great Recession. Some consumers have had monies of which they were cheated restored. But all this consumer protection and punishment the bureau has been achieving is now in peril. Elements in Congress who want to allow the banks and credit card companies to resume the very profitable deception and exploitation of consumers have waged an effective campaign to make the Bureau ineffective.

At this point it looks as if they will be successful in destroying the authority of the bureau. So consumers may soon be finding themselves again at risk from the same unscrupulousness that created the recent economic crisis. You are warned.

Basic Precaution: Read The Fine Print

Some basic common sense precautions will help you avoid problems. Only take out a loan when you absolutely must. Be realistic about how much you will be able to regularly repay. Ask yourself a lot of what if such-and-such happens questions. If you must take out a mortgage or a loan, pay it off as soon as possible. Be sure to read and understand every word of any document you sign— loan, lease, anything.

My insistence on this first word to the last word reading has insulted and annoyed lawyers, leasing agents and numerous others who shoved a document under my nose with the expectation that I would sign based on their explanation of the terms of the document. Nonetheless, I have always read before I signed. And in those readings I have found errors and imprecise wordings that could have caused problems later.

But I always give fair warning so that reading time can be scheduled prior to the signing. Two days before closing on this property I bought in 2009, I phoned the woman at the title company who would be directing closing procedures. I told her of my reading policy. She said their were 67 documents to sign. I said with less than 48 hours till signing, I needed to get started.

Within 30 minutes she had emailed PDFs of all the documents. I began reading. On the appointed day, I arrived at the closing with a list of five points about which I had questions—and the blue gel pen recommended for signing legal documents. My questions were answered satisfactorily in less than 15 minutes. The blue gel pen and I did our duty to the 67 documents. Possible problems—at least thus far—have been avoided.

Connoisseurship Requires Money

For even the savviest connoisseur, outfitting yourself for chic takes money. Quality clothes and accessories range from reasonable to "with the same amount of money you could buy a small island." Skilled hairdressers and aestheticians value their work and charge accordingly. Staying slim takes money. High quality food costs more than poor quality. (Highest rates of obesity are among those of lowest income. Lowest rates of obesity are among the best-educated and higher income.) Staying safe costs money. Secure neighborhoods and good quality schools raise the price of real estate. To be chic, slim, and safe will mean that if not rich, at least you must be financially secure. On this fourth, the three previous depend.

The Facts Total And Clear

The foundation of your connoisseur success is accurate information. But getting the truth and the full picture is not easy these days. A deluge of information—good, bad and imbecilic—continually washes over us. Much of that information is purposely deceptive and misleading. Some of it, only inadvertently so. Above all else we must become connoisseurs of the information we use to make the decisions about our lives.

What NBC News Technology columnist Wilson Rothman advised about protecting yourself from smartphone malware today applies equally to life in general:

It pays to be a little paranoid—and a lot informed.

The You Factor

BEAUTY IS IN the eye of the beholder. One person's trash is another person's treasure. For the *Chic & Slim* Connoisseur, quality is determined by how well it serves the user's needs.

As for beauty, as for your possessions, ultimately quality must be judged by its relationship to *you*.

The technology experts may all rate a cellphone the absolute best. But if, of its 94 features, you only use five, and if you have to consult the user's manual every time you check your voice mail, a simpler phone would be the better quality for you.

A pair of 100 percent wool pants might be exquisitely tailored. But if they are dry clean only and you live 26 miles from the nearest dry cleaning shop, and it is difficult for you to find time to take the pants for cleaning, the better choice for you might be a machine washable synthetic blend.

The majority of you reading this book will not have unlimited funds to buy the best quality for *everything* in your life. You will have to set priorities. If you have a long daily commute through demanding urban traffic and your boss is totally intolerant of lateness, for you, a quality vehicle will be a greater priority than for a retiree who only drives to shopping, church, the hairdresser and volunteer work.

You will surely be wise to consult experts and other users whose needs and lifestyle are much like yours. In the end, however, you should not permit other people to define the best quality for you.

The *Chic & Slim* Connoisseur knows: The best person to define the best quality for you is *you*.

Recipes

A HOUSEHOLD MAINTAINED by servants—including a French-trained cook. For me, those days are past. Today most convenience foods are not quality. So, like most of you reading this book, to enjoy quality meals, I must cook (and clean up). In everything I prepare I strive for delicious taste and good nutrition, as well as quick preparation and cleanup. On the following pages, I share several of my recipes—and one of my mother's: her 1950s favorite Baked Chicken Spaghetti mentioned in the Slim section.

As I wrote in that Slim section, when I was growing up in the 1950s, Chicken Spaghetti was my mother's frequent choice when a meal needed to be prepared in advance for guests. Our budget was tight and the dish was economical. Guests always loved it.

Helen's Baked Chicken Spaghetti

1 hen, (about 4 lbs.) stewed	1 box spaghetti
1 large onion, chopped	2 cups celery, finely cut
1 green pepper, chopped	1 cup pitted ripe olives, sliced
Salt and pepper to taste	Dash of cayenne pepper
1 cup rich chicken broth	2 cups tomato juice
1 can mushroom soup	2 bay leaves
1 Tbs. Worcestershire sauce	Grated Parmesan cheese

Stew the hen until tender. Cool in the broth. When cool enough to handle, remove skin and bones. Sauté the onion, celery, and green pepper in cooking oil until soft, add tomato juice, chicken broth, Worcestershire sauce and soup, stir well. Add bay leaves and cayenne. Simmer for 30 minutes uncovered. Cook the spaghetti and drain.

In a large casserole, layer the chicken, spaghetti, and vegetables. Bake at 350 degrees F. for 30 minutes. This chicken, pasta and vegetable combination should be moist, but not soupy. If it becomes dry while baking, add more chicken broth. Can be prepared a day ahead, refrigerated and then baked just before serving. Also freezes well.

The secret to flavor in this dish is allowing the stewed hen to cool in the broth before removing the skin and bones. Of course, my mother's recipe did not include instructions for cooking the hen nor the spaghetti. It assumed anyone following the recipe would know how to properly stew a hen, or at least owned a basic cookbook in which one could find the instructions. It also assumed that anyone could follow the cooking directions on the box of spaghetti. It did not specify size of box because our grocery store sold only one size box of spaghetti. "Rich chicken broth" means that the fat has not been removed. The only Parmesan cheese available to us in the 1950s was the Kraft version, but I would not recommend it if you can possibly buy real Parmesan or Romano cheese.

The recipe serves 10. For a larger crowds, the recipe would be doubled or tripled as needed. My mother often served chicken spaghetti with a green salad and garlic bread, large loaves of the American version of "French bread" sliced diagonally, spread with butter blended with minced garlic, wrapped in aluminum foil and heated in the oven 10 to 15 minutes immediately before serving. Oily on the fingers, but delicious. Homemade chocolate or applesauce cake often followed the main course.

Anne's Updated Baked Chicken Spaghetti

It has been a half century since the days guests ate my mother's chicken spaghetti with such gusto. Today we have nutritional concerns that did not trouble us in the 1950s. We also have food products unavailable in our grocery stores when my mother was preparing this dish frequently. For my *Chic & Slim* lifestyle, I have updated my mother's chicken spaghetti recipe to make it more nutritious and more flavorful. Preparation time remains essentially the same. Like my mother, I think chicken spaghetti is best accompanied by a green salad. For me, however, the spaghetti is sufficient starch for a meal. I skip the bread. If you wish to include bread in your meal, I would suggest an Italian style bread. For dessert to follow the chicken spaghetti, I would choose something lighter than cake, probably a lemon or lime sorbet.

1 4-lb free range chicken	Water
1 16-oz. box multigrain spaghetti	
1 28-oz. can of diced tomatoes	
2 tablespoons olive oil	2 cups yellow onions, chopped
2 cups celery, sliced	1 green pepper, sliced
1 teaspoon dried OR 2 teaspoons fresh oregano	
8 ounces fresh button mushrooms, cleaned and sliced	
6 cloves fresh garlic, crushed	1 cup pitted ripe olives
1 Tbs. Worcestershire sauce	1 cup chicken broth
1 tablespoon flour	Salt and pepper to taste
1/2 cup Italian parsley leaves	Pecorino Romano cheese, grated

Rinse the chicken and put it into a large pot and cover with water. Bring to boiling, lower heat, then simmer until chicken is tender, about 2 hours. Cool the chicken in the broth. Take the chicken out of the broth and remove skin and bones. Cook the spaghetti according to package instructions. While spaghetti cooks, sauté the chopped vegetables in the olive oil about

10 minutes, add the tomatoes with their juice and liquid ingredients and simmer for 25 minutes to reduce the liquid. Mix a little of the hot liquid into the flour and blend. Add the flour paste to the vegetables and stir well to blend. Simmer 5 minutes to thicken.

In an oven-safe casserole, layer chicken, spaghetti and vegetables. Bake covered in a 350 degree F. oven for 30 minutes. Can be prepared a day ahead and baked immediately before serving. Depending on the shape of the casserole, if the dish comes straight from the refrigerator, it may require 10-to-20 additional minutes to heat properly. Keep some of the chicken broth on hand to add to the casserole if it becomes dry during baking. When ready to serve, scatter the Italian parsley over the top. Offer Romano or Parmesan cheese to garnish. Serve with green salad.

Anne Barone's Soupe Verte

Hardly a week goes by that I don't make a pot of this healthy soup. Whole milk plain yogurt stirred into the hot soup immediately before serving gives this green soup a creamy good taste. Add a chunk of hearty bread or a couple of Swedish rye crispbread crackers, and you have a satisfying meal.

1 bunch kale

1 yellow onion, chopped

4 cloves garlic, peeled

1/2 teaspoon dried marjoram

2 tablespoons olive oil

2 chicken bouillon cubes

2 to 3 cups water

Wash the kale and remove thick stems. Chop the onion. Peel and crush the garlic. Sauté the onion in oil 5 to 10 minutes. Stir in the kale and garlic and marjoram. Add the water and bouillon cubes. (You can, of course, substitute real chicken broth, if you have it.) Cook until greens are tender, about 30 minutes. Cool slightly. Puree in blender. Return to pan and reheat to a simmer. Serve soup topped with 2 tablespoons to 1/4 cup thick plain yogurt.

Flax Seed Bread à la Barone

This bread recipe is designed for a 2-pound loaf made in a home bread machine. It will work equally well made by conventional bread making methods. I divide the dough into two loaves and bake in two 3 x 7 x 2-inch loaf pans inherited from an aunt. These pans make smaller size loaves perfect for tea sandwiches.

1 1/2 cups plus 2 tablespoons water

2 1/2 cups bread flour

1 cup whole wheat flour

3/4 cup ground flax seeds

1 teaspoon salt

2 1/4 teaspoons (1 pkg.) instant yeast

Using a blender or food processor, grind the flax seeds to a flour consistency. (Or use flaxseed meal.) Put the ingredients in the pan of the bread machine according to the directions for that machine. Use the Basic Bread setting, the one that takes approximately 3 hours from start of mixing to end of baking. For conventional oven method, bake in preheated oven at 400 degrees F. Baking time will depend on the size and shape of loaf or loaves. You can buy ground flax seeds sold as meal or "milled flax seed," but it is usually more economical to grind the whole seeds at home. To measure home-ground flax seeds, pack lightly in measuring cup and level.

Barone Potager Spring Salad

You might call it a pre-*potager*. Early last spring, before I completed the frame of my little backyard French style kitchen garden and filled it with good soil, I established an area planted with spring greens in the long narrow flower bed that runs across the back of my little house. I bought nine spinach plants and nine lettuce plants at the plant store and set them out. An onion had sprouted before I used it for cooking. I stuck that in the ground too. Common blue violets grow profusely in my garden. While not all flowers are edible, these dainty blooms are. Since I use no pesticides or chemicals in my yard, they are safe to eat.

Within a week and a half of planting, my lettuce and spinach plants were growing sufficiently well that I could begin taking some outside leaves for salad and leaving the main part of the plants to continue to produce. These early pickings became the basis for a lunch salad. Below are ingredients and directions.

Spinach leaves

Lettuce leaves

Green tops of onion

Violet blossoms (optional)

Feta cheese

Olive oil

Lemon juice,

Dijon mustard

Salt

White or black pepper

With kitchen shears or scissors snip off a few outer leaves of the spinach and lettuce plants leaving the main part of the plant. Cut one or two green tops of onion. Gather violet blossoms if using. (Make certain you gather only the common blue violet that is safe to eat. Verify that no pesticides or chemicals have been used in the area it grew.) Wash all well. Pat dry. Cut spinach and lettuce into bite-sized pieces. Snip onion greens into thin slivers and sprinkle over leaves. Crumble on feta cheese. Make a vinaigrette whisking 1 part lemon juice in 2 parts olive oil. Add 1/2 teaspoon prepared Dijon mustard such as Maille or Grey Poupon for each tablespoon of lemon juice. Pour vinaigrette over greens. Remove the stems from the violet blossoms and scatter the blossoms over the salad. Use only 4 or 5 violets per serving.

This salad tastes delicious eaten with French-style baguettes or flax seed bread. For a more substantial meal, serve this salad with grilled chicken breasts or fish fillets.

Connoisseur Nasturtium Tea Sandwiches

Nasturtium tea sandwiches have long been a favorite nibble for my afternoon tea. Easy to make, they are also beautiful and elegant. I prefer to gather the leaves and blossoms early in the morning when freshest. Wash and put stems in water to keep fresh until teatime.

Nasturtium leaves and blossoms *(I grow mine from Burpee seeds.)*

Thin slices bread

Butter, cream cheese or tahini

Salt

At teatime, cut thin slices of bread, removing the crusts if you prefer. Spread the bread with butter, cream cheese, or tahini. Salt lightly. Cut bread into halves or fourths. Wash well and remove stems from nasturtium leaves and blossoms. Place 3 nasturtium leaves and 2 blossoms on half the bread pieces. Top with another piece of bread. You can also make elegant open-faced sandwiches with nasturtiums. Cream cheese makes a pretty base for the colorful flowers.

These sandwiches are delicious served with Darjeeling tea. My very favorite tea for these sandwiches is a pricey Indian tea, the first flush organic Darjeeling from the Makaibari Tea Estate. For the best taste of this "sweet, floral, sophisticated" tea, steep for a full 5 minutes as instructed by Rajah Banerjee, the tea estate's owner. His excellent organic and biodynamic teas, Fair Trade policies and respect for the environment make this tea one that meets *Chic & Slim* Connoisseur standards of quality.

Creating Family Food Legacies

The food industry increasingly sells us what *The Omnivore's Dilemma* author Michael Pollan aptly calls "edible food-like substances" instead of real food. For economy, and for healthy, slim bodies, a savvy connoisseur will increasingly find quality must be created by their own efforts. *Potagers*, kitchen gardens, can provide quality, convenience and delicious taste. Become an *artiste de cuisine*. Nothing in a packaged industrial faux food or carryout box equals the delicious taste that our own kitchen artistry creates. Besides, in preparing meals from our own personalized recipes, we are creating family food legacies, a rich inheritance we leave our children.

Connoisseur Thoughts

JUST AS I WAS completing this book, I received an email from one of the *Chic & Slim* women who told about her frustration in trying to buy a quality jar of jam. Lisa in Seattle wrote:

> During my visit yesterday to the gourmet market, I picked up a small $5.00 (on sale) jar of jam for my morning bread. Unfortunately, I neglected to check the label, as I thought an item so costly would be free of high fructose corn syrup. Well, I was wrong!! I am so frustrated with the garbage that these companies put into their food!!!!!!!!!!! No wonder Americans have so many health problems, obesity being high on the list. At least with fast food a person knows what they are getting, but to stick junk into "higher quality" foods just irritates me to no end!! I understand more each day how you feel. As a busy society, we should not have to "police" food like we do and the ability to obtain healthy food should be available to us all.

Many of us are feeling this frustration today. We who have learned the chic French lessons for slim know the necessity of quality products. But identifying and finding quality just gets harder and harder.

This book was written to help make this important task easier so you can continue to make the French-inspired *Chic & Slim* techniques I have given you in the previous *Chic & Slim* books work for you.

Another email arrived earlier in the summer. Yucchi at The Nanny Speaks Out blog wrote:

> Your book arrived, I already devoured it! And reread it too!. . .

In many ways I feel as if you are reminding us of things we know deep inside but we need the reminding and the validation to follow through.

Mais, oui! Much I write in the *Chic & Slim* books is time-tested common sense. Yet because of the barrage of advertising, or peer pressure, or what someone—perhaps someone with less than pure motives—is pressuring you to do, you don't trust yourself to do them. So, yes, the reminding and validation.

Life brings many hard but valuable lessons. Every day I am aware of how much that I now know, that had I known these truths and techniques earlier in my life, I could have been spared much pain, frustration and disappointment. I could have achieved much more success in my career and personal life.

My *Chic & Slim* books are my sincerest and best effort to share with you the valuable lessons that I have learned and continue to learn. My aim is that you have the greatest *savoir faire* so that you may be spared as much pain, frustration and disappointment as possible—and that you may have the greatest success and *joie de vivre*.

Become a *Chic & Slim* Connoisseur so that you can use your knowledge and experience of quality to become chic, slim, safe and rich—in your own unique personal style.

be chic, stay slim
Anne Barone

About Author Anne Barone

Once fat and frumpy, in her mid-20s Anne Barone began to learn chic French women's techniques for eating well and staying slim—and for dressing chic on a small budget. She lost 55 pounds and acquired a chic French wardrobe.

Chicer and slimmer, Anne Barone returned to the USA to find a nation growing sloppier and fatter. She decided to share her French secrets.

In 1997, Anne Barone published her first French-inspired book *Chic & Slim: how those chic French women eat all that rich food and still stay slim*. More *Chic & Slim* books followed.

In her books, and on *annebarone.com*, the *Chic & Slim* companion website, Anne Barone continues to share French secrets for dressing chic and staying slim.

Now in her late 60s, she has stayed slim for more than 40 years.

Anne Barone lives in Texas where she is attempting to create a bit of French Provence on the North Texas plains. "Far enough in the country to grow eggplant, apricots and lavender. But close enough to Dallas to make the sales at Neiman Marcus."

Chic & Slim Books & Info

Chic & Slim:

How Those Chic French Women

Eat All That Rich Food And Still Stay Slim

Chic & Slim Encore:

More About How French Women

Dress Chic, Stay Slim

—and How You Can Too!

Chic & Slim Toujours:

Aging Beautifully Like Those Chic French Women

For more

Chic & Slim Connoisseur

Information & Resources

visit the *Chic & Slim* supporting website

annebarone.com

be chic
stay slim

CPSIA information can be obtained at www.ICGtesting.com
Printed in the USA
LVOW07s2107121213

365049LV00037B/1249/P